NASCAR
2000

THE EVOLUTION OF
SPEED

ACKNOWLEDGMENTS

It is with great pleasure that UMI Publications, Inc., in conjunction with Street & Smith's Sports Group, R.J. Reynolds Tobacco Company and NASCAR, presents "NASCAR 2000: The Evolution of Speed."

This book documents perhaps the greatest success story in the history of American sports: the evolution of NASCAR racing. We take you from NASCAR's roots more than 50 years ago to the sophisticated sport we see today by covering its drivers and champions, the cars, the tracks, and the constant application of technology. Then, we take a peek into the future to present some of the many exciting developments fans can expect that will make NASCAR racing even more enjoyable than ever. We've also included a special section you are sure to love – a chapter dedicated to NASCAR's wonderful fans, including many of your own photographs sent to us to illustrate your dedication to this great sport.

This book would not have been possible without the combined efforts of many dedicated people. Our very special thanks go to our friends at Street & Smith's Sport Group, Whitey Shaw, Kirk Shaw, Steve Waid, Tom Jensen, Ben White, Art Weinstein, Mark Ashenfelter and Jeff Huneycutt for providing the text and photos that comprise the bulk of this publication. Thanks also to veteran photographers Phil Cavali, Jim Fluharty, Bambi Mattila and Tim Wilcox for opening their files to supply us with so many fine images to illustrate this book.

Special appreciation goes also to David Chobat, who dug deep into his photo archive to help us document many special moments in NASCAR history. In addition, a very special thank you to Buz McKim and Daytona Racing Archives for supplying so many significant photographs dating back to the earliest days of NASCAR.

Without the support of the NASCAR Winston Cup Team at R.J. Reynolds Tobacco Company and Sports Marketing Enterprises this project would not have become a reality. Our thanks to Rick Sanders, Greg Littell, John Powell, Larry Prillaman, Steve Ticker, Mike Fagan, Dennis Dawson, Mitch Cox, Mary Casey, Denny Darnell, Mark Rutledge and Chad Willis.

We would also like to extend our gratitude to our good friends at NASCAR, who provided valuable guidance and support in making this book. To Bill France, Jim France, Brian France, Lesa France Kennedy, Mike Helton, Paul Brooks, George Pyne, Kelly Crouch, Jennifer White, John Griffin, Paul Schaefer and the rest of the NASCAR staff go our deep appreciation.

Finally, special thanks to you, the fans. It is your continued support that makes the phenomenal story of NASCAR's success possible. So, to you we dedicate "NASCAR 2000: The Evolution of Speed."

Please enjoy.

UMI Publications Staff

Ivan Mothershead, President and Publisher; **Charlie Keiger,** Vice President and Associate Publisher; **Rick Peters,** Vice President; **Lewis Patton,** Controller; **Mark Cantey,** National Advertising Manager; **Paul Kaperoris,** Advertising Account Executive; **Ward Woodbury,** Managing Editor; **Merry Schoonmaker,** Senior Associate Editor/ Production Manager; **Michael Kruse,** Senior Editor/Collegiate Sports Division; **Brett Shippy,** Art Director; **Paul Bond,** Senior Designer; **Chris Devera,** Manager of Information Systems; **Mary Flowe,** Customer Service Representative; **Linda Goltz,** Customer Service Representative; **Heather Guy,** Customer Service Representative; **Joanie Tarbert,** Customer Service Representative

Preproduction work provided by ISCOA (International Scanning Corporation of America). Printed in Willard, Ohio through RR Donnelley & Sons Company.

ISBN # 0-943860-17-2

TABLE OF CONTENTS

FOREWORD

It's hard to believe.

Over 50 years ago, a group of men led by the redoubtable William H.G. "Bill" France, formed an auto racing sanctioning body they called the National Association for Stock Car Auto Racing. Its mission was to organize the rambunctious sport of stock car racing by establishing rules, competing at selected venues, awarding drivers prize money and ultimately, crowning a true national champion. At the time not even France could have envisioned the evolution of NASCAR.

From half-mile dirt tracks where the dust could create a brown haze, NASCAR now races at glittering speedways all across the country; speedways of all shapes and sizes that boast the finest in amenities.

From hulking brutes of cars that were not far removed from the showroom floor, today we have sleek, colorful machines; so aerodynamically sound and powerful they are capable of speeds unimagined when NASCAR was born.

NASCAR's first drivers were hardy and courageous. Most of them raced for the enjoyment of it; few made a living at it. Today, NASCAR's drivers are still hardy and courageous. They rank among the most popular of all professional athletes and have acquired skills not needed by their predecessors. They have become as competent at interacting with fans, sponsors and the media as they are behind the wheel. And, yes, they make a living doing something they love.

NASCAR has been a pioneer in the development of race car safety. It has been a process that has come a very long way from the days when a driver, wearing jeans and a T-shirt, belted himself into his car with a rope. Today, NASCAR's race cars are considered the safest in motorsports, constructed so well and equipped with special devices to protect the driver – who now wears a fire-retardant uniform, protective helmet and other safety apparel.

Where NASCAR was once considered a regional sport enjoyed by a relative few and virtually absent from the airwaves, it is now enjoyed by millions of fans from coast to coast. National television networks broadcast every race.

It's hard to believe. But it's true.

This book, "NASCAR 2000: The Evolution of Speed," will make that abundantly clear to you. It is the premier book on the changing face of NASCAR; a record of its history and a glimpse into what lies ahead in the new millennium.

Inside you will find dramatic photos and informative text that will bring into focus the development of NASCAR's race cars. You'll also learn the lineage of its drivers, from the pioneers to today's stars, to those who will lead NASCAR into the future. You'll see how NASCAR's races progressed from wood-and-nail speedways carved out of fields to palaces of speed. You'll discover how technology advanced, and the benefits it brought to NASCAR, its teams and drivers – and how it made the sport safer and more exciting.

There's much more in "NASCAR 2000: The Evolution of Speed." It is the perfect record of NASCAR's past, its present and where it may go in the future.

Enjoy "NASCAR 2000: The Evolution of Speed." After you do, you will reach the same conclusion:

It's hard to believe.

A

DURING THE 1982 NASCAR WINSTON CUP SERIES SEASON, WILLIAM HENRY GETTY FRANCE (LEFT) PAUSES FOR A MOMENT OVER TWO OF THE

SOPHISTICATED

GREATEST ACCOMPLISHMENTS OF HIS LIFE: THE FORMATION OF NASCAR AND THE STORIED 2.5-MILE DAYTONA INTERNATIONAL SPEEDWAY.

SPORT

ABOVE, RICHARD PETTY WAS THE MOST RECOGNIZED PERSONALITY ON THE SPORT AS IT MATURED THROUGHOUT THE 1960S, '70SAND '80S.

In the very beginning, the words "sophistication" and "stock car racing" didn't seem to fit in the same sentence.

But one man deeply wanted them to.

His vision was to create a sport respected by all as a legitimate, competitive venture.

He died in 1992 after a lengthy illness before seeing his dream come to full fruition and too soon to fully realize what he had created some 44 years earlier.

From the moment Bill France Sr. began to envision forming an alliance for racing stock cars off the showroom floor in the years after the conclusion of World War II, one point was first and foremost: there needed to be a crop of talented drivers who could keep the turnstiles spinning, but could also manage themselves before a curious but often judgmental public. After all, if his fledgling organization would ever be respected as a legitimate national sport, a solid relationship with the fans would have to come first, while professionalism would have to be the name of France's game in order to attract early corporate sponsorship.

(Above) Curtis Turner (No. 26) leads Tim Flock (No. 15) during the Convertible event of Feb. 16, 1957 at Daytona Beach. Flock won the race while Turner came in 13th out of 28 cars entered. (Left) Joe Weatherly sits ready to go in his 1956 Ford prior to the Beach and Road Course event held on Feb. 26 of that year. Unfortunately, the Virginia native eventually suffered problems and finished 44th in the 76-car field.

*Three top finishers of the first Southern 500 at
Darlington Raceway hold a special place in motorsports
history. They are, from left to right: third-place finisher
Fireball Roberts, second-place Red Byron and race
winner Johnny Mantz.*

Some of the very first NASCAR races were held on the 2.2-mile Daytona Beach and Road Course when the sport was officially formed in 1948. One could be sure the competition would be keen, the surf and the sands would be deep. Red Byron (No. 22 at far left) goes around the struggling Mickey Rhodes (No. 26) and Marshall Teague (No. 6) being bogged down in ruts created by the starting field.

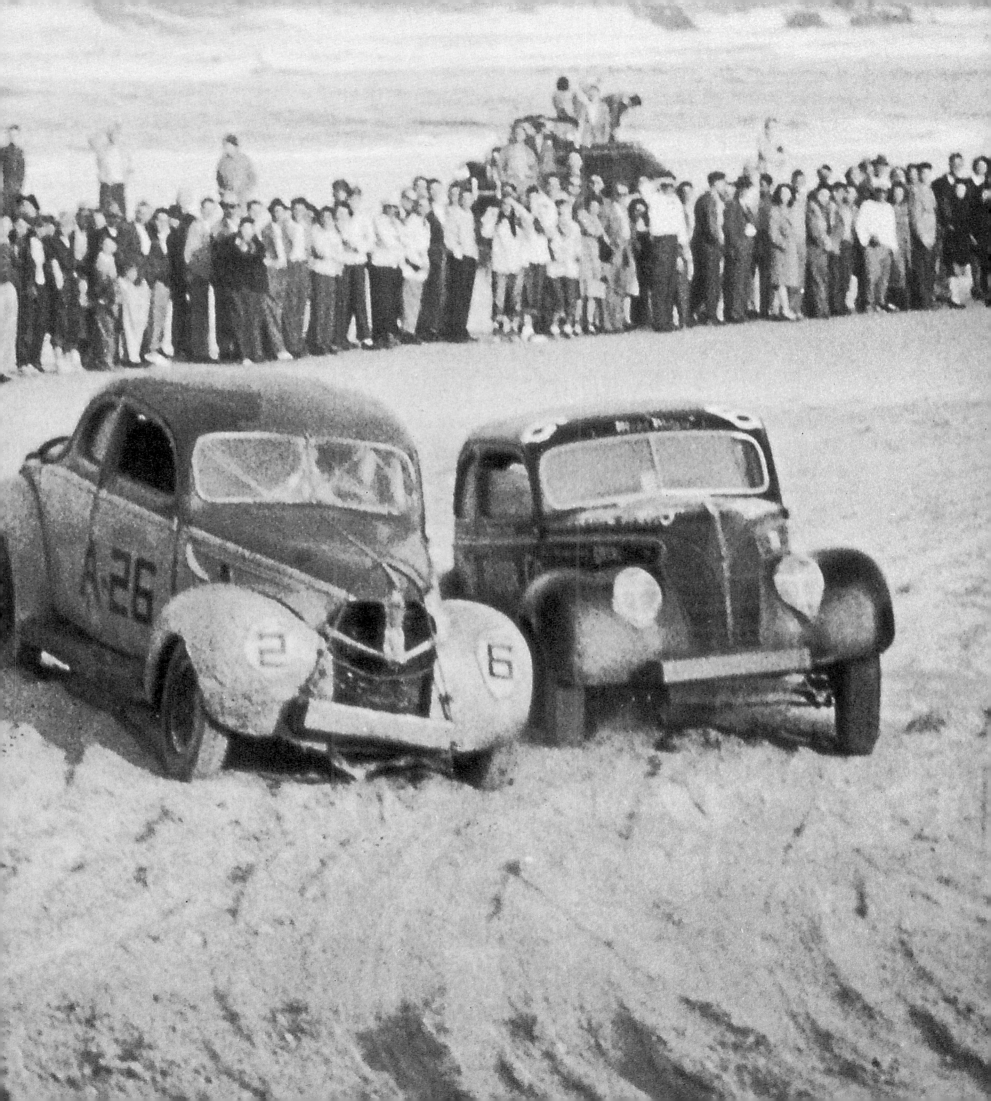

Family has always been a part of NASCAR. There have been the Pettys, the Allisons, the Bakers, the Jarretts, the Bodines, the Wallaces, and so may more throughout the sport's 52-year history.

"All you have to do is just look as far as the Pettys and you see several generations of family racing in the sport," Kyle Petty says. "My grandfather Lee started and ended his career here at Petty Enterprises. My father Richard started and ended his career here. I plan on ending my career here someday. It's important to us as a family because this is what we do. We've had a race team for 50 years. We've won races and been competitive, and now, fifty years later, we're still competitive and can still win races. That's important."

"To be able to build it back like it was in the late 1960s and early '70s is what we want to do," Richard says. "That's our goal, whether we do it with Kyle, or whoever comes along, it doesn't make any difference. The point is to get back to being a contender every week."

The numbers are favorable for families in the sport as well. The Pettys have 263 wins, the Allisons 113, Earnhardts 77, Jarretts 73, the Flocks 63, Wallaces 50, Labontes 34, and the Bodines 18.

Lee Petty (Opposite page left), twice a NASCAR Grand National champion, shows Goodyear's Blue Streak special to a very young Richard Petty, later a seven-time NASCAR Winston Cup Series champion, at the tire's introduction in 1960. They became the first father-son champions when Richard won his first title in 1964. (Above) Another seven-time champion, Dale Earnhardt (No. 3), shows the ropes to son Dale Jr. early in the 2000 season, the younger Earnhardt's first full year in the NASCAR Winston Cup Series after winning two consecutive titles in the NASCAR Busch Series, Grand National Division. (Right) Brothers Tim Flock (left) and Fonty Flock are all smiles before the start of a NASCAR Grand National event in the late 1950s.

NASCAR Winston Cup Series regular Bobby Hamilton stands alongside his son, Bobby Hamilton Jr. The younger Hamilton is currently using the NASCAR Busch Series, Grand National Division as a way to set the foundation for his future NASCAR Winston Cup Series career.

Brothers Bobby Labonte (left) and Terry Labonte have been a fixture in the sport for many years. Combined, they have won 34 races with championships going to Terry in 1984 and 1996.

Ned Jarrett retired from race driving in 1966 after winning championships in 1961 and 1965 and 50 races. His son, Dale Jarrett (right), made them the second father-son champions when he won the title in 1999.

Tim Flock is joined in victory lane at Hickory, N.C., on May 16,
1953, by wife Frances and five children. Flock was the reigning champion at
the time, having been crowned NASCAR Grand National champion in 1952.
He captured the title again in 1955.

(Above) As the 2000 season opened, brothers Darrell (left) and Michael Waltrip had 1,176 NASCAR Winston Cup Series starts between them, with older brother Darrell tied for third (with Bobby Allison) on the all-time wins list with 84 and three NASCAR Winston Cup Series crowns. (Right) Coo Coo Marlin (left) encourages his son Sterling to follow in his footsteps as a race driver. Sterling, who was once a crewmember for his father in the early 1970s, now has nearly 500 starts and six victories, including two Daytona 500 wins.

Three generations of Pettys stand proud for a brief moment together on March 20, 1999. Kyle, (far left) his father Richard (center) and Kyle's son Adam represent the winningest family in NASCAR history. Sadly, Adam lost his life in an accident during a practice session at Loudon, New Hampshire on May 12, 2000.

One of the most prominent families in NASCAR history are the Woods, of the famed Wood Brothers Racing team, which began fielding NASCAR Grand National cars in 1953.

Brothers, Glen (standing at left) and Leonard, founded the family-run operation, which continues today under the daily direction of sons Len and Eddie. In the photo above, the Wood Brothers are presented The Spirit of Ford Award by Ford Motor Company in 1999. Pictured are (from left) Terry Hall, Kim Wood Hall, Len Wood, Eddie Wood, Edsel Ford, Bernece Wood, Glen Wood, Beth Witt and Leonard Wood.

(Above) Bobby Allison (left) finds a quiet moment with younger brother Donnie Allison, in the late 1970s. (Right) Ricky Rudd poses with his wife, Linda, and son Landon, for a family portrait.

Fonty Flock (No. 1) puts his machine far out front and enters the South Turn in the first NASCAR event at Daytona Beach on Feb. 15, 1948. Flock led 60 miles of the race and was in the lead with 18 laps to go when a front spindle broke. Flock flipped his '39 Ford and finished 19th.

Joe Weatherly (12) speeds past Jimmy Thompson in the Convertible Division event at Daytona Beach in 1956. Weatherly won the pole position, but he eventually settled for 19th place in the 28-car field.

When France ventured south from his native Washington, D.C., to the beaches of Florida to capitalize on their wide-open spaces available for racing in 1934, Miami was his original destination. But fate placed him in Daytona Beach, where he and his wife Anne stopped along the way. They loved Daytona Beach and decided to stay. He eventually opened his own filling station and affectionately referred to it as the place where local racers gathered to talk about upcoming races and the ones just completed. It was France's vision to bring together and organize stock car racing once and for all under one recognized sanction.

For four days in December of 1947, France assembled various businessmen with strong interests in racing from different parts of the country and formed the National Association for Stock Car Auto Racing. There were no parades or brass bands playing when the name "NASCAR" was transformed from mind to paper. On February 21, 1948, NASCAR was officially incorporated and well on its way.

The initial races in NASCAR history were held on makeshift dirt arenas around the Southeast, as well as annual events at Daytona on what was known as the Beach and Road Course, labeled as such for the track that was made up of the sands of Ponce Inlet south of Daytona Beach and Highway A1A.

Red Byron poses with his winner's trophy after driving to victory at Daytona Beach on Feb. 15, 1948. Byron went on to become NASCAR's first stock car champion at the end of the 1949 season.

A full starting field in the Strictly Stock division prepares to take the green flag at the three-quarter-mile dirt track known as Charlotte Speedway on June 19, 1949 in the first NASCAR sanctioned race.

Billy Carden (No. 8) puts his Lincoln out front with another Lincoln behind and a 1950 Ford to his left on the Beach and Road Course at Daytona in 1951. These early cars had few modifications from their normal stock trim.

Jim Paschal (No. 17) and Frank Schneider (No. 45) lead the field on a restart during the 1957 Beach and Road Course race. Paschal finished 45th in the 57-car field, while Schneider finished 40th.

Thanks to another visionary, Harold Brasington, France had the first piece of motor-sports real estate from which to build. Some 18 months after NASCAR was formed, the first super-speedway was in the fold, Darlington Raceway in Darlington, S.C. At the hands of its builder, the hard working Brasington, 1.25 miles of asphalt and high-banked turns covered the middle of a former cotton field. While many of the town's people thought he bordered on crazy, newspapers from across the South were intrigued by such a phenomenon — a track originally planned after the master open-wheeled arena, the Indianapolis Motor Speedway.

The tract of land where Darlington Raceway was later constructed begins to take shape in what was once a 70-acre cotton field. Note the first and second turns (left) are narrower in radius than turns three and four. The reason was to save a minnow pond outside of turn two that had to remain as part of the agreement between Brasington and former owner Sherman Ramsey, the man who traded the land for stock. While Brasington spent nearly a year building the track, Ramsey spent his time fishing the pond.

Fans from all walks of life came to Darlington that hot September day in 1950 to see Johnny Mantz take an underpowered Plymouth to victory lane in the 75-car field. Having such a speedway on which to hold events gave France a large boost in becoming established as a front-runner among several small racing sanctions that continued to crop up.

(Above) The starting field for the inaugural Southern 500 on Sept. 4, 1950 is three cars per row to accommodate the 75-car starting field. (Right) Johnny Mantz hugs the winner's trophy after winning the first Southern 500. His mount for the six-hour marathon was a 1950 Plymouth.

Drivers such as Curtis Turner, Jim Paschal, Lee Petty, Glen Wood, Red Byron, the Flock brothers, Bob, Fonty and Tim, and a young Fireball Roberts were establishing themselves as NASCAR's initial stars.

Throughout the decade of the 1950s, Darlington remained the mainstay superspeedway and acted as a finale of sorts on a long schedule of short tracks. But France had another speedway in mind, the largest facility to date that spanned longer and wider than any other.

(Opposite page) The huge crowd on hand at Charlotte for the inaugural NASCAR event in June 1949 watches Lee Petty charge down the frontstretch in his Buick.
(Above) The 75-car field charges into the first turn on the first lap of the inaugural Southern 500 on September 4, 1950. The crowd that came to witness the historic occasion was much larger than expected, and fans quickly filled the infield after the grandstands had reached their capacity.

By the start of the 1960s, France's biggest accomplishment had been open for business for the better part of a year: the 2.5-mile Daytona International Speedway. With its opening, drivers graduated to a new form of superspeedway racing. It was the largest configuration of any kind NASCAR's new fans and new stars had ever seen.

Seven-time NASCAR Winston Cup Series Champion Richard Petty remembers seeing the track that seemed to go on forever. Eventually, the Randleman, N.C., native would win seven Daytona 500s there during his 34-year career.

(Left) Richard Petty charges under the flagstand in 1964 to win his first Daytona 500. Five years earlier, his father Lee accomplished the same feat in the first running of NASCAR's biggest race. (Below) On January 11, 1972, Big Bill France hands the keys to Daytona — and to NASCAR — to his son, Bill France Jr.

The ever-popular Joe Weatherly cracks a huge smile for the camera in his No. 12 Ford convertible at Daytona in 1956.

"When we rolled in there in 1959 and I saw that track for the first time, it was the biggest place I think I had ever seen," Petty says. "When I first went through the tunnel there was really nothing there — no buildings and no fences. They had a guardrail around the track and some grandstands. But the place was humongous.

"We had been racing at Darlington, but Daytona was really something to see. It was so new there was just a lot of dirt and a lot of new asphalt all over the place. It was quite a sight to see for a bunch of cats who had spent most of their time racing short tracks. It definitely opened some new doors for us drivers. No doubt about that. No one had ever seen anything that big before, anywhere."

By the time Petty won his first Daytona 500 in 1964, his father Lee (1959), Junior Johnson (1960), Marvin Panch (1961), Fireball Roberts (1962) and Tiny Lund (1963) had all been victorious in the prestigious 500, the biggest event in stock car racing. To win it meant sure exposure among the media outlets of television, newspaper and radio. Lee Petty and Johnny Beauchamp were involved in a photo finish in the first Daytona 500 with Petty being awarded the win days after the checkered flag fell. The exciting finish gave France something to sell to the public for the 1960 Daytona 500.

"Some of the battles Curtis Turner and Joe Weatherly had on some of the small dirt tracks were legendary," Richard Petty recalls. "But a cat that came and gave this thing a boost when it needed it was Junior Johnson. That was when he was still a driver. There wasn't a Chevrolet out there that was competitive in the early 1960s, but Junior took an old 1963 Chevrolet and won a lot of races with it. He would either win in that old white No. 3 Chevrolet or tear off all the fenders and doors on half the cars in the field trying. That's what made the fans come back the next week and that's what the sport needed.

Curtis Turner pilots the No. 41 Wood Brothers Ford in 1966. Although much more sophisticated than the Strictly Stock cars of the 1950s. The cars of the '60s were still modified showroom vehicles. Notice the door handle, stock bumpers and chrome trim around the windows.

Junior Johnson, driving the Ray Fox-owned '63 Chevrolet, edges in front of Fireball Roberts during the 1963 Firecracker 400 at Daytona. Roberts was driving a Holman-Moody Ford and picked up four wins in his 20 starts that year. Johnson made 32 starts for Fox in 1963 and drove to victory lane seven times.

"Junior Johnson, Curtis Turner, Fireball Roberts, Joe Weatherly and David Pearson — those guys were racers. They would tear the fenders off their cars doing it. That's the only way they knew how to race."

In the early years, the sport wasn't very fan friendly as compared to the present. Only the top stars seemed to be approached for comment, and picking the right time to ask was the key to a good interview.

"The problem with Fireball Roberts and Fred Lorenzen was that they were very good when you called them at the right time," says Bob Moore, a veteran motorsports writer for more than 40 years. "But when you called them at the wrong time, they were not overly friendly.

"Fireball was the first guy who understood that part of his job was to answer very well and very smartly when a newspaper or television guy asked what Fireball believed to be a dumb question. He felt like it was his job to educate the race fans, and he did it through the media."

Curtis Turner holds the victory trophy with car owner Peter DePaolo after winning the Convertible Race on the Beach and Road Course in February 1956. On DePaolo's right is second-place finisher Fireball Roberts. (Right)Hard-charging David Pearson stands in front of his Cotton Owens-owned Dodge at Daytona in 1966. It would be 10 years before Pearson would win his only Daytona 500, although he scored five victories in the Firecracker 400, including three straight from 1972-74.

Others took very little seriously, especially those fun-loving types who couldn't wait to spill a funny quip.

"Curtis Turner and Joe Weatherly had a lot of fun together," Moore remembers. "They enjoyed playing with the media. So while the media came to Fireball because he was the star, it came to Curtis and Joe and because they had a good time. The writers would know they would get some off-the-wall quotes."

NASCAR lost Roberts, who gained his nickname from baseball and not racing, on July 2, 1964, after an accident at Charlotte in May of that year. Roberts was set to retire from the sport at the end of the season to work in public relations representing a major corporation. Many felt the sport had lost its greatest spokesperson through which positive images of NASCAR were presented to the public.

Fred Lorenzen sits focused, ready, before going to work in the Motor Trend 500 at Riverside in January 1964. Lorenzen's NASCAR career spanned form 1956 to 1972, during which he scored 26 wins and 84 top-10 finishes in only 158 starts. (Opposite Page) Fireball Roberts stands ready to climb into the 1963 Holman-Moody Ford for the '63 running of the Firecracker 400 at Daytona. Roberts won the event, his second straight and his third in the five times the summer classic had been run.

Colorful Tiny Lund sizes up the competition before the 1963 Firecracker 400. Lund, who also drove a Holman-Moody Ford in the event, had his best season that year, finishing 10th in the final point standings.

Richard Petty poses at Daytona with one of his famous
Plymouths of the early 1970s. Petty's name became synonymous with
winning at Daytona during the '70s; He won four of his seven Daytona
500s and one Firecracker 400 over the decade.

In 1967, Richard Petty and Petty Enterprises once again heavily promoted the sport by logging 27 victories in a single season with 10 coming consecutively. With that type of success occurring at any given speedway during the 60-race schedule, Petty gained great exposure and helped France keep the stands filled. Most came to the track just to see if he could chalk up one more win, like Babe Ruth swinging for one more home run. Each time he fired his engine, he seemingly gained more fans in the process.

Moore believes Petty helped the sport more than any other in the years when the fans were deciding if stock car drivers were athletes or just crazy for traveling at such high speeds. Petty's contributions are so numerous they are hard to measure.

"Richard Petty was the best, and still is by far," Moore says. "There was no one in Richard's class and that's still true today. If there had been no Richard Petty, and no one who understood his total role from the viewpoint of the race fans and the media, this sport would not be where it is today. I can't understate that fact. Richard basically elevated this sport beyond where it could have been. Darrell Waltrip elevated this sport. Dale Earnhardt elevated this sport in the 1980s, but in the 1960s and 1970s, if Richard Petty had not existed, we wouldn't be where we are today. Richard Petty helped the sport when the sport needed help the most."

(Above) Richard Petty picked up his second Daytona 500 win driving this 1964 Plymouth. Three years later, Richard would win a record 27 races, including his incredible string of 10 in a row that earned him the nickname "The King." (Right) In 1965 at Darlington, the Chrysler drivers lined up for this "team" photo, including Lee Petty (center standing) with young Richard by his side. The team concept was not totally new, with manufacturers actively involved in supporting their drivers with parts and mechanical assistance.

Richard Petty waves to the crowd after winning the 200th race of his career on July 4, 1984 at Daytona. Looking on is Ronald Reagan, President of the United States, and Bill France Jr., president of NASCAR.

Along with Petty, another group of drivers were at the forefront of the headlines, such as Bobby Allison, Donnie Allison, David Pearson, Buddy Baker and Cale Yarborough, to name a few. But the sport was still considered regional and only a few newspapers were willing to give precious space in their sports pages for stock car racing. Major sponsorships from such corporations as Coca-Cola, STP, Purolator and Carling Beer were finding their places on the quarter panels of the cars at the front of the field. Still, public relations representatives were far from the norm.

"The big change was really through the 1970s and into the 1980s," says Bobby Allison, the 1983 NASCAR Winston Cup Series champion. "About the middle to late 1980s, the rules began to get really well defined. The competition continued to get better and better. The cars now are very similar to the 1988 cars. The chassis — the old front-steer cars that I liked so well — are still going and are the best things out there. A lot of little things have been tried like that. The engine development has also gotten better. The engines we used would get 525 to 550 horsepower. Now, they have close to 800 horsepower. Same engine, same size, same carburetor and all that."

In his day, Allison was one of the fortunate ones who could use his talent to keep his name etched on the rooflines of some of the best cars. As time went on, the level of competition became stronger with each passing season.

In 1969, Ford put together this all-star team that included (counterclockwise from left) Richard Petty, Cale Yarborough, David Pearson, Donnie Allison and LeeRoy Yarbrough. In the season's 54 events, Ford led the way with 26 wins, including LeeRoy's sweep of both races at Daytona.

"The competition has gotten so much deeper," Allison says. "Everybody can get the good information and everyone has to run by the rules that are so well defined by NASCAR. As a result, there are 45 cars that can run competitively with each other right from the very beginning. It used to be you would have six or eight really good cars, and there might be 10 or 12 medium cars. Those 10 or 12 might get things together on a given day to get through the pack to the front. Then you would have maybe 20 cars that really had no chance of winning, but they were good competitors and put good-looking vehicles out on the race tracks — machines that would be appealing to the eyes of the race fans.

"In 2000, every car out there potentially could win the race and are capable of winning the pole position for any given race. The NASCAR Busch Series is exactly the same. That's what seems to be fueling the fans' true respect and love for NASCAR these days. They just can't seem to get enough of it, and their interest in the drivers they read about now is pretty incredible.

Harry Gant (left) and Bobby Allison have a laugh together during the 1982 season. In his fourth full year in the NASCAR Winston Cup Series, Gant broke into the win column with a season sweep at Martinsville.

"There's more money — not just money for one person. It's money for everyone who wants to be involved and who fields a team. Anyone who really puts the effort forth can find some kind of financial help. If they can run well at all, then they can find decent financial help. If they run really well, then they get the really big dollars. And the big dollars are there."

When discussing races of the 1970s, it was a select few drivers who kept NASCAR's elite division at a fever pitch. They were the catalyst of a sport that battled a national energy crisis in 1974 and the problem of larger cars on the race tracks when the consumer trend was leaning more and more toward smaller cars.

The decade of the 1970s was in many ways the bridge to the future. Had it not been successful with legendary races that helped gradually build ticket sales, the sport may have folded — or at least taken a different direction.

"We, meaning myself, David Pearson, Cale Yarborough, Buddy Baker and Richard Petty, developed what is now known as the Modern Era," Allison says. "There were a lot of other drivers who set the foundation of the sport in the 1950s before I ever got in a car. But in this phase, starting with the middle 1960s and especially the early 1970s and on into the 1980s, we really built what we see today, and I'm proud to have been a part of that. We went there and raced hard for whatever we could race for, and we earned whatever we could and were happy with that. From there, we went on our way and tried to promote NASCAR racing as much as we possibly could. It has grown into an incredible industry, and I'm just proud to have had a hand in developing it."

"The bottom line is, the thing has been a product of team effort," Allison says. "It's tough trying to get there, but there's always a team who works a little harder to get better than the guys next to them. That's happened in NASCAR forever, and that's the thing that has made the sport so strong and so attractive."

(Above) Curtis Turner, driving the No. 13 Smokey Yunik-owned Chevrolet, holds off Cale Yarborough's Wood Brothers Ford during the 1966 National 500 at Charlotte. (Right) Buddy Baker won only once in 1970, but he made it count by driving to victory in the prestigious Southern 500 at Darlington. Here, Buddy (far right) shares the spoils of victory with members of his crew, sitting atop their 1969 Dodge Daytona - one of the first cars developed primarily for stock car racing, and one of the most fascinating cars ever to compete in NASCAR.

The association to the American automobile is the biggest asset for NASCAR. As with any chosen occupation, one must have transportation to get there, and identifying with what's on the track continues to make the sport popular. Just like the 1960s when the slogan "Win on Sunday — Sell on Monday" was prevalent, the same holds true today. Some feel that's why the highly technical world of open-wheel racing suffered over the past decade.

"Everybody rides in a car and can relate to the automobile," Allison points out, "so that's what turns the fans on so much. The fans are thinking something like, 'Wow, that's my favorite kind of car.' Or they might imagine that if they were out there racing, they wouldn't let a certain guy go around them. That really keeps the fans turned on, and it also keeps the consumers sponsor-loyal for years to come."

Through the 1970s and most of the '80s, all drivers were considered a driver's driver, as the machines they drove were big and cumbersome compared to the technical, well handling machines of today. To take a heavy Dodge Charger or Mercury Montego or Chevrolet Malibu and race for 500 laps around a place like Bristol Motor Speedway was considered miraculous by today's standards.

(Above) The Fords of Fred Lorenzen (No. 28) and A.J. Foyt battle it out at Atlanta in April 1964. Street cars heavily modified for racing, these stockers still bore a strong resemblance to the cars purchased and driven by loyal fans, and the Ford dealers would be ready for business the next day after Lorenzen notched the win. (Right) Cale Yarborough wheels his bright red Galaxy, a car that inspired many enthusiastic fans over the late 1960s.

(Above) LeeRoy Yarbrough puts his Dodge Charger on the low side to hold off Cale Yarborough in the Wood Brothers Ford during the 1966 National 500 at Charlotte. Battles between marques on the race track fueled fierce loyalties among fans and added an additional layer of competition to the sport. (Left) After little participation in the 1950s and only limited success in the early '60s, Mercury rolled out the Montego model in 1968. Drivers Cale Yarborough (No. 21) and LeeRoy Yarbrough, battling here in the 1968 Daytona 500, were a potent combination, leading the manufacturer to seven wins during the season, including a Daytona sweep by Cale.

"The cars were harder to drive in the older days," says 1989 NASCAR Winston Cup Series Champion Rusty Wallace. "There's no doubt about that. When we had the bias-ply tires I would get out of the car completely worn out.

"I recently talked with Dale Earnhardt about a race we once had at Bristol. I passed him, he passed me, and this went on all day. It was a hundred degrees, and when it was over I just slid out of my car. He pulled into victory lane and he was so weak he kept reaching up to hit the switch to turn off the motor, and he kept missing it because his arms were so numb and tired. We were just absolutely exhausted.

"Now, with power steering and new seats and all that, it's not as hard physically as it was in the old days. Heaven help those guys like Bobby Allison and Cale Yarborough and the older guys like that who ran the races at Bristol with no power steering while using bias-ply tires. Those are some tough dudes. We're a bunch of wimps compared to those guys."

To train for such events, Allison would turn the heat switch in his car to high and roll the windows tight on a scorching hot Alabama summer afternoon. When asked what he did to stay in shape to drive a race car, longtime driving veteran Dick Trickle has said, "Just that. Drive a race car." Physical stamina was required of drivers much more so than today, but drivers still train and use their body strength as an advantage when fighting with so many competitive cars.

"You have to remember it was what you were up against at that time," Wallace says. "You were all on equal terms. No one had power steering and you never thought about how hard it was. When you look back at it, it was pretty hard.

"These days in NASCAR Winston Cup racing, you have to know your car. You've got to know you're shocks, your springs and know what the race track does. That's what makes you good."

Wallace isn't one to work out on a regular basis, but does do exercises for certain parts of his body that are most affected, such as his neck for tracks like Bristol Motor Speedway, Daytona or Talladega.

Ned Jarrett carried the Ford banner over the late 1950s and early '60s, picking up 50 wins over seven seasons. At top, Ned wheels his very handsome Ford during the 1965 Daytona 500, the year he claimed his second NASCAR championship. (Right) A fierce competitor on the track, Ned's endearing smile and friendly demeanor eventually helped him make the transition to the broadcast booth after his retirement in 1966, where he quickly became a favorite personality and fine spokesman for the sport.

Dale Jarrett is strapped in and ready to go in the Joe Gibbs Racing
Chevrolet at Atlanta in 1994. The year before, Dale picked up the biggest victory
of his career to that point by winning the Daytona 500 to the delight of millions
watching on television as father Ned called the thrilling final laps from the
broadcast booth.

The Wood Brothers Racing crew fits their driver Marvin Panch with tires and fuel at Charlotte in October 1963. Treaded tires carried over a guardrail from pits in the dirt were the way it was done nearly 30 years ago.

Fireball Roberts takes a cool drink while his Ford receives service along Charlotte's pit road in 1963.

"I don't really work out all that much," Wallace says, "maybe every two weeks or so, mostly to work with my neck muscles. But these cars have power steering and are built much better now. They aren't as hard to drive as cars of 25 years ago."

Noted crew chief and team manager Buddy Parrott came into the sport in 1970 and has seen it progress handsomely over the past 30 years. When improvements came in the pits, excitement was generated among fans wanting to see tires being changed in record time.

"The sport really has changed dramatically," Parrott says. "I remember back in the days of working with the late Harry Hyde. In 1973, we set the world's record for the Union 76 Pit Crew championship. The record was to change two tires in 21 seconds. Now we change four tires in the 15-second bracket. Today, the crews practice three times a week. The equipment is better. The jack is better. There's a lot of engineering that goes into racing now. That's been the difference.

"As far as getting physically prepared for a race, we didn't do much of that 30 years ago. Now, the crew members train for body strength and flexibility — things like that. That's a big factor.

"I started changing tires when I first became a crew chief in 1975. I changed the right-front tire just out of necessity. But I loved to do it and continued to do it through 1990 when I was with Derrike Cope (the Daytona 500 winner that year).

"It's a young man's sport. A guy who is in his mid to late 30s, he's just about considered over the hill."

A Holman-Moody crew member prepares the pit board to signal their driver during the 1963 World 600 at Charlotte.

In stark contrast to years gone by, pit crews today are
highly specialized, well equipped and carefully trained to perform
their tasks flawlessly. The precious fractions of a second that are
gained and lost on pit road can easily translate into winning – or
losing – at the end of the race.

(Above) The world championship-winning pit crew for
Bobby Labonte shows their stuff at Talladega. Every move by every
crewman is carefully orchestrated and rehearsed like a high-speed
ballet. (Right) Unlike the T-shirts and jeans worn in the past,
crewmen are outfitted specifically for their jobs – always with
safety in mind. Dale Earnhardt's gas man and catch-can man both
wear protective fire suits and helmets, complete with built-in radio
communications. Notice how the crewman on the right steadies
the catch can with one leg while holding the 85-pound fuel can in
perfect position. (Below) With a NASCAR inspector observing the
work on every pit stop, there is no room for error. A loose lug nut,
errant air hose or tire left unattended on pit road will surely result
in a costly penalty.

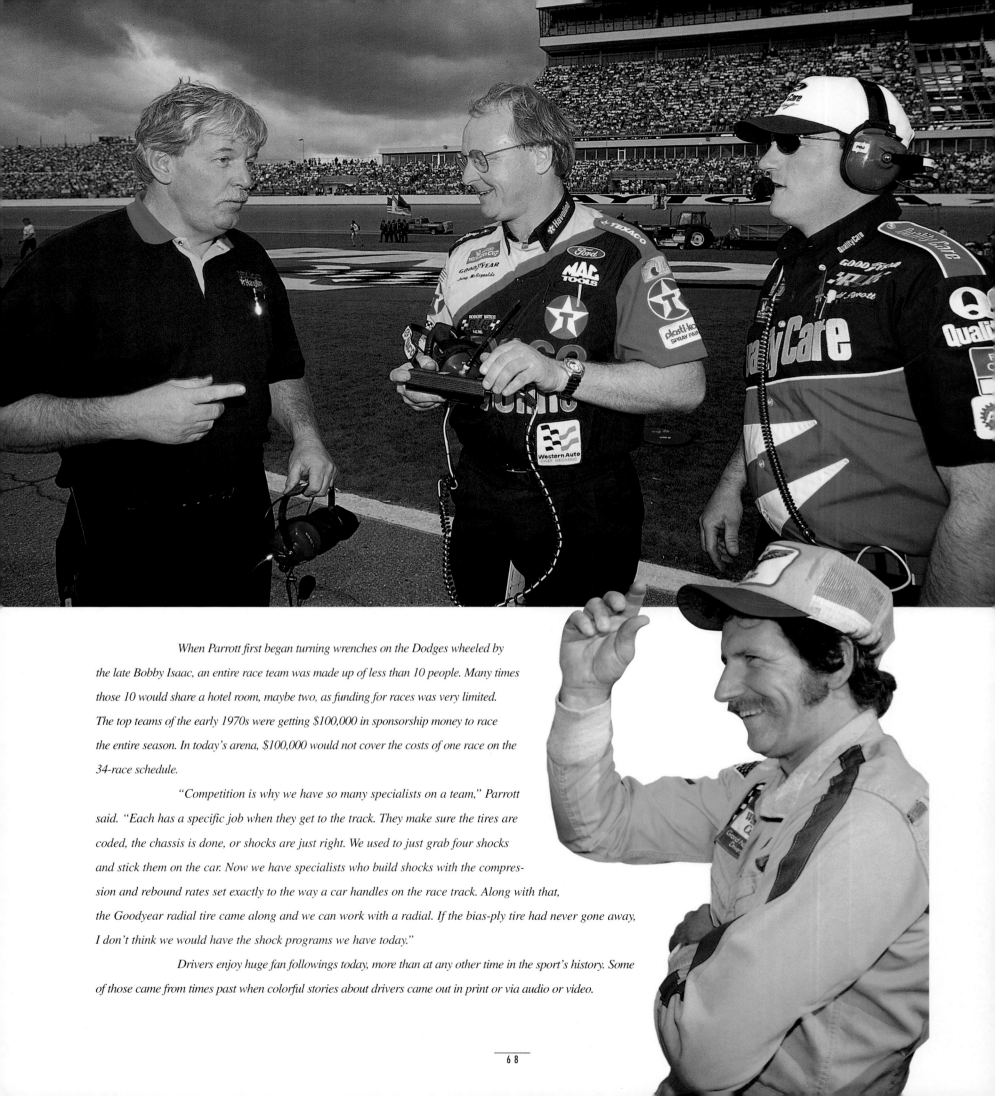

When Parrott first began turning wrenches on the Dodges wheeled by the late Bobby Isaac, an entire race team was made up of less than 10 people. Many times those 10 would share a hotel room, maybe two, as funding for races was very limited. The top teams of the early 1970s were getting $100,000 in sponsorship money to race the entire season. In today's arena, $100,000 would not cover the costs of one race on the 34-race schedule.

"Competition is why we have so many specialists on a team," Parrott said. "Each has a specific job when they get to the track. They make sure the tires are coded, the chassis is done, or shocks are just right. We used to just grab four shocks and stick them on the car. Now we have specialists who build shocks with the compression and rebound rates set exactly to the way a car handles on the race track. Along with that, the Goodyear radial tire came along and we can work with a radial. If the bias-ply tire had never gone away, I don't think we would have the shock programs we have today."

Drivers enjoy huge fan followings today, more than at any other time in the sport's history. Some of those came from times past when colorful stories about drivers came out in print or via audio or video.

One of the colorful aspects of NASCAR Winston Cup Series racing was the fact that "head games" could be played between drivers that would have some strong impact on the outcome of the race. Whether Darrell Waltrip was razzing Cale Yarborough, or Bobby Allison was taunting Richard Petty, their words of wisdom would most certainly get around, making life a bit stressful at times.

"It's a distraction to be honest. That's what it all boils down to," says Waltrip, a three-time NASCAR Winston Cup Series champion. "You never really intend to be mean or vicious or unkind. It's just a way to get another team derailed in their efforts to win a championship.

"If you could get a guy mad at you or upset with you, sometimes it would make him race differently. It would make his crew react a little differently to you. If you could get his team solely focused on you and not what everyone else was doing, that was part of the plan. We would get the other driver and his guys so upset with us and so focused on what we were doing, they might make mistakes. They'd quit working on their car and start looking at your car. They'd be so aggravated with you, they would race only you and think only about you."

Do mind games work in the 1990s? Many feel with the constant corporate image that's being portrayed, there's no room for it. But it does make for great headlines.

"You can play mind games today just as well as you could back then," Dale Earnhardt says. "If you got close to another team in points, you could start working on them.

"Darrell and I, and other guys over the years, have worked on each other. But I don't know that drivers like Jarrett, Gordon, Bobby Labonte, have been pulling at each other. There's a lot of respect among the top teams."

(Opposite page above) Team owner Robert Yates (left) has a light moment with his crew chiefs, Larry McReynolds (middle) and Todd Parrott, just before race time. In today's high-stakes, pressure-packed environment, times like these are valued – and appreciated. (Opposite page left) Dale Earnhardt tips his hat at Ontario, Calif., as he closes in on his first championship in 1980. His total winnings that year were less than $600,000 – roughly the equivalent of his winner's check at the 1995 Brickyard 400. (Above) NASCAR Director Dick Beaty (left) plays mediator to Darrell Waltrip (center) and A.J. Foyt in the mid-1980s. Two of the masters in the philosophy of competition, Waltrip and Foyt could play the "mind games" as well as anyone in the sport. (Left) Cale Yarborough celebrates his qualifying record set at Charlotte for the 1980 World 600, one of 14 poles he collected during the year to set a record that has yet to be broken.

Drivers such as Dale Earnhardt and Darrell Waltrip began to overshadow the older veterans and saw the need to use the media to draw them closer to the fans. Both were hard charging and outgoing, on and off the race track.

"The way they can deal with the media and the public is what has changed the most about NASCAR drivers," Moore says. "Outside of Richard Petty and Ned Jarrett, both NASCAR Winston Cup (then Grand National) champions, the drivers basically didn't do a lot with the public. Even in the media, it wasn't that strong. Part of the reason is that in the mid 1960s to the early 1970s, there were only four or five newspapers that covered racing on a daily basis. The drivers knew those reporters pretty well. But at Daytona or Charlotte or maybe Atlanta, there would be a lot of media there that the drivers didn't know. The big difference in drivers now is how much better they are at talking to the media and to the general public — the race fans."

(Below) Among the drivers known for his ability to interact with fans is Bill Elliott, as evidenced by his astounding domination of NASCAR's Most Popular Driver Award. Elliott has received the honor every year but two since 1984 – those going to Darrell Waltrip – including a consecutive string that dates back to 1991. (Right) Perhaps the most sought-after person in the NASCAR garage over the past 20 years by fans and media alike has been that of seven-time champion Dale Earnhardt. Here, Dale finds a secluded spot in front of his team's hauler to grant an interview with television reporters.

A significant contribution came in 1971 when a major corporation stepped up to the plate to be the Series' title sponsor and help NASCAR bring it center stage.

"A major part of turning around the drivers' mentality regarding the media was through R.J. Reynolds Tobacco Co.," says Moore, a former public relations representative for the company. "In the early 1970s, they made a conscious effort to deal with the media a lot more. RJR did a lot to help publicize the sport and to make the drivers stars. Then, CBS showed the 1979 Daytona 500 live flag to flag, and then ESPN came along and started bringing weekly television coverage to racing. Between RJR and all of the television coverage, the drivers had to learn to work with the media, and had to learn the importance of public relations. That later spilled over to the crew chiefs, as well. All this helped to make the drivers more likable and accessible to the fans. That's what seems to be giving NASCAR its biggest growth — the fact that drivers are human and they can relate to the fans who support them."

As the 1980s came to a close, it was a time when corporate America would begin to see NASCAR as a market to showcase the country's most popular products. No longer were automotive brands the predominant primary sponsors being displayed on the cars.

In today's arena, one is likely to see any type of sponsor imaginable — everything from camera film to breakfast cereal to a prescription drug for men. Huge corporate dollars have finally come to the sport and made Bill France's Sr.'s dream of having a legitimate professional sport known as NASCAR come true. Those large corporate sponsorships have helped bring the sport to fans in new markets across the country.

"Exposure to the new fans is certainly one of the biggest changes," says Barney Hall, the longtime anchor of MRN radio. "Obviously we are going from one coast to the other now. The thing that blows my mind is how many fans show up every week for a race. That's just unreal when you stop and think about it.

"Look at Bristol Motor Speedway for instance. You just want to question how they can have that many seats around a half-mile, high-banked speedway, and fill them up each and every time they hold an event."

To bring fans closer to the drivers and sponsors was the ultimate goal of R.J. Reynolds when it joined NASCAR some 30 years ago.

"I talked about that very thing with the late T. Wayne Robertson of R.J. Reynolds Tobacco Co.," Hall continued. "Their goal, from the time they came into it in 1971, was to penetrate new major markets and take it away from being a regional deal. They wanted more than just North Carolina, South Carolina, Georgia and Tennessee. They worked on that, and NASCAR also had the foresight to move it to some other new markets. I think that's why we are where we are today.

(Opposite page) Jeff Burton grabs his $1 million check after victory in the 1999 Coca-Cola 600 at Charlotte, a bonus offered through Winston's No Bull 5 program. Celebrating with Jeff is car owner Jack Roush. Burton leads all drivers, having collected the million-dollar prize three times since the program came into effect for the 1998 season. (Above Right) When NASCAR raced at Indianapolis for the first time in 1994, the $600,000-plus winner's share paid to Jeff Gordon was unheard-of, far surpassing any other event on the tour. Since then, checks ranging from a half-million to more than a one million dollars have become far more common. Gordon pushed his Indy winnings to nearly $2 million after the fifth running of the Brickyard 400 in 1998 by becoming the first two-time winner of the event. (Above) By taking the Indy win in 1997, Ricky Rudd collected the largest check of his career – a whopping $571,000 for his day's achievement.

"No one person made this happen — got us to where we are today. It took a bunch of people, from a Ralph Seagraves (RJR Tobacco Co.), to a Bill France, to a Junior Johnson, to a Richard Petty — you could go on and name 50 people that had a big part in getting NASCAR racing to where it is in 2000."

At one point, the fans were asking where their new stars would come from. Bobby Allison retired after an accident in 1988, while Cale Yarborough called it quits the same year. David Pearson quit in 1989. Petty retired in 1992, as did Buddy Baker. The stars that everyone had loved and followed for decades were gone. The fans needed someone new.

(Opposite page) Without the vision and guidance of the late Bill France Sr., the many and varied careers and success stories that have been created through the sport of NASCAR racing simply would not have been possible. (Top) Junior Johnson (left) discusses some mechanical points with Bill France Jr. at Daytona International Speedway's garage area in the early 1980s. As a team owner, Johnson was a true innovator, a fact that led to six NASCAR Winston Cup Series championships – three with Cale Yarborough (1976, '77 and '78) and three with Darrell Waltrip (1981, '82 and '85). (Right) As the 1992 season draws to a close, Richard Petty passes his "crown" to son Kyle. A week after this photo was taken, Richard retired as a driver. During his career, The King made 1184 starts, with 200 wins, 555 top fives and 712 top-10 finishes.

Tony George (right), president of Indianapolis Motor Speedway, shares a laugh with Bill France in 1993. By working together, the two men reached an agreement that brought the NASCAR Winston Cup Series to the famed Speedway in August 1994, fulfilling the dreams of many. (Right) Roger Penske (left) engages in a discussion with Bruton Smith during the 1996 season. At the time, the two men owned six of the 19 venues on the NASCAR Winston Cup Series schedule, with Smith controlling Atlanta, Bristol, Charlotte and Texas, while Penske owned Michigan and California in addition to his NASCAR Winston Cup Series race team with driver Rusty Wallace.

"I think it was the late 1980s when they started moving forward to where we are today," Hall says. "There was a shortage of drivers. There was a lot of talent in the NASCAR Busch Series and people were looking for outside guys, but there just weren't any.

"They brought in a few guys from other forms of racing, but they didn't make it. So a lot of team owners built NASCAR Busch Series cars. Then they would put a Busch driver in it and if he performed well, they got to move up to NASCAR Winston Cup.

"Credit Bill France for making the NASCAR Busch Series cars more like NASCAR Winston Cup cars in the late 1980s and early 1990s, so drivers wouldn't have such a tough transition going from the NASCAR Busch Series cars to the heavier NASCAR Winston Cup machines. That's probably why guys like Jeff Burton, Tony Stewart and Dale Earnhardt Jr. have come from the NASCAR Busch Series and immediately started winning in NASCAR Winston Cup."

Humpy Wheeler, president of Lowe's Motor Speedway, has a keen eye on all of the up-and-coming competition from various forms of auto racing.

"Both Jeff Gordon and Tony Stewart came from open-wheel backgrounds, and both started racing when they were very young," Wheeler says. "Jeff moved up faster than Tony and obviously, Tony is developing later.

"The Sprint Car experience has helped them tremendously because of the dirt racing they did. It helped them because NASCAR Winston Cup races are usually run in warm weather and the track is going to become greasier as the day wears on. The cars get looser, and a lot of drivers fall straight back when the tracks gets slick.

Two-time IRL Champion Tony Stewart waits for service to be completed on his Indy car during the 1999 Indianapolis 500 (top). One of the few drivers to make a smooth transition to stock cars from the open-wheel ranks, Stewart put together the most successful rookie season in NASCAR history in 1999, scoring three late-season wins and finishing an outstanding fourth in the final point standings. (Opposite page) As a teenager, Jeff Gordon became a fixture in victory lane driving Sprint Cars throughout the Midwest. He discovered stock cars while attending a driving school, and the fit was so natural, he began racing in NASCAR events almost immediately. In a few short years, Gordon had scored 50 wins and three NASCAR Winston Cup Series championships, all before the age of 30.

"You look at Dale Earnhardt when he was in his prime, he came to the front when the track started to deteriorate. Jeff goes to the front in those conditions and so does Tony. I think that should be a wake-up call to anyone thinking of a career in NASCAR Winston Cup racing."

In the year 2000, many new faces are coming into the fold. There's Dale Earnhardt Jr., Matt Kenseth, Johnny Benson, Tony Stewart and Steve Park, just to name a few. It's the best time to be in NASCAR, as the fan base continues to grow with each race, each season and each coveted championship. Without a doubt, it is the fastest growing spectator sport in America.

"I think being a driver in NASCAR in the year 2000 and seeing where we're going is pretty awesome," says Johnny Benson, driver of the MB2 Motorsports Pontiac. "I'm sure NASCAR isn't at the top quite yet because there still room to grow. It's neat to be involved with all the different types of sponsors, all the different types of race fans, and the different types of race tracks and towns we go to. Right now, I'm extremely happy to be in the NASCAR Winston Cup Series.

"I think the sky is the limit. This is only my fifth year and I've seen the changes that have happened. I've seen the changes over the past 10 or 15 years, and if we can accomplish just a percentage of the growth NASCAR has already enjoyed, our future still holds tremendous change."

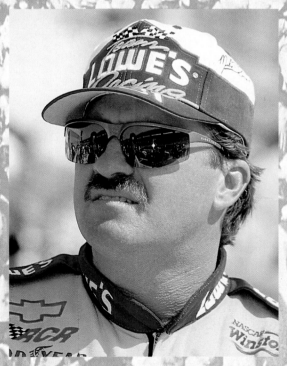

(Opposite page) The son of a NASCAR legend, Dale Earnhardt Jr. made it stock cars from the very beginning. After learning the ropes in the Late Model ranks and making just nine NASCAR Busch Series starts over two seasons, the younger Earnhardt began to dominate, winning two consecutive NASCAR Busch Series championships in 1998 and 1999. As a NASCAR Winston Cup Series Rookie of the Year contender in 2000, "Little E" scored his first big league win in only his 12th career start, besting all other drivers in NASCAR's Modern Era – including his dad. (Above) With the 2000 NASCAR season, it's evident the competitiveness that made the sport so popular among fans is at an all-time high, with championship contenders such as (top from left) Bobby Labonte, Jeff Burton and Ward Burton, facing the challenges of bright new stars such as (bottom from left) Matt Kenseth, Scott Pruett and Mike Skinner.

SPEED AND

(LEFT) HARRY GANT POPS HIS OLDSMOBILE UP ON TWO WHEELS AFTER CUTTING A CORNER SHORT.

SAFETY DRIVE

DON'T TRY THIS WITH YOUR FAMILY CAR. (ABOVE) TAKE AWAY THE PAINT AND DECALS,

STOCK CARS

AND RUSH HOUR AT TALLADEGA MIGHT LOOK LIKE YOUR USUAL RIDE HOME ON THE INTERSTATE.

The year is 2025, and a rookie NASCAR Winston Cup Series driver is nervous ... *s debut in the upcoming Daytona 500. So he heads to his race shop, dons a helmet and climbs* ... *he wheel of his race car. His crew chief plugs in a computer program and for the next several* ... *he rookie will "drive" the Daytona 500, with the computer simulating the event in incredible* ... *including the roar of his own engine, the smells of the race, and 42 other "virtual" drivers* ... *to pass him.*

Sound impossible? As NASCAR stands on the brink of a new century, that's just one of ... *azing innovations that may be waiting down the road.*

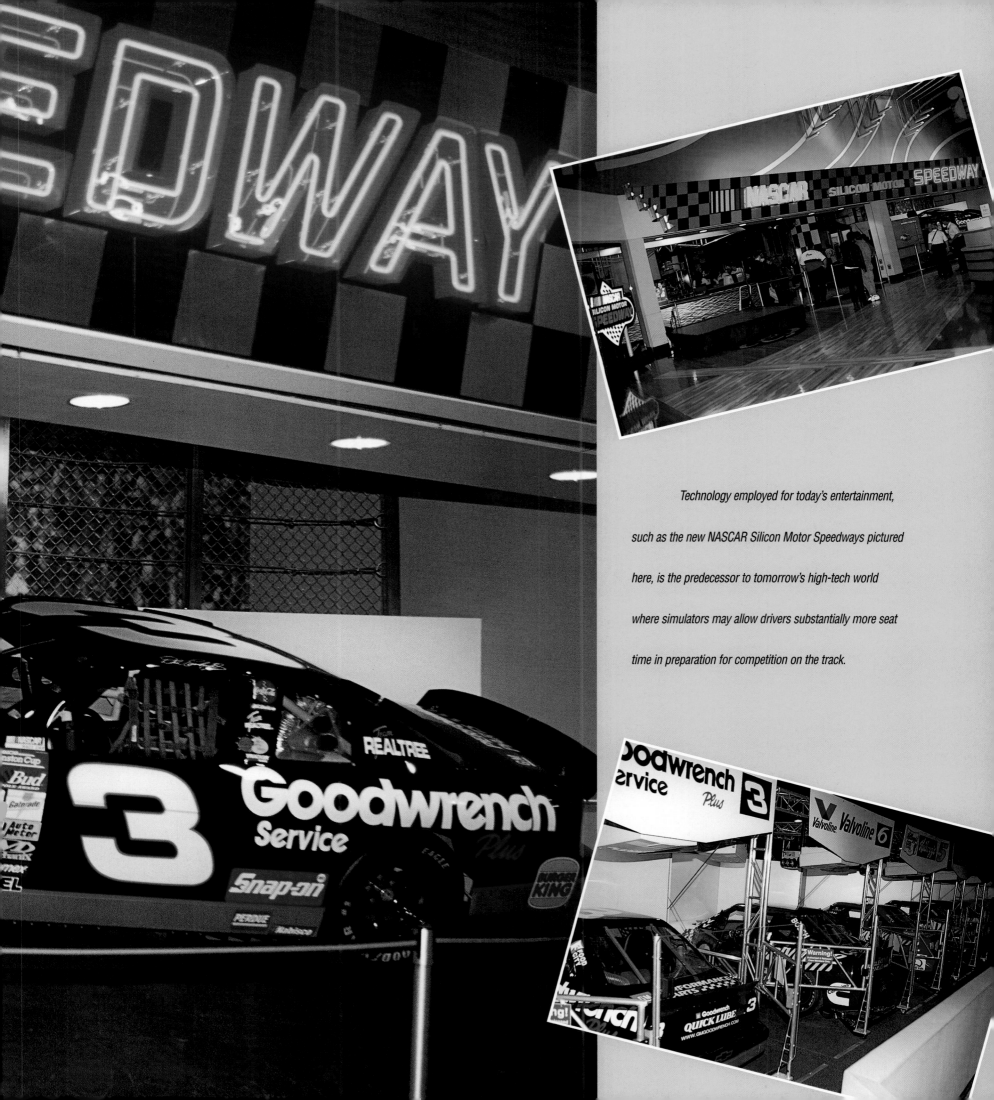

Technology employed for today's entertainment,

such as the new NASCAR Silicon Motor Speedways pictured

here, is the predecessor to tomorrow's high-tech world

where simulators may allow drivers substantially more seat

time in preparation for competition on the track.

Five decades of NASCAR race cars graphically illustrate the evolution of change in the sport. Note how the cars have become progressively more streamlined, illustrating both changes in designs from Detroit automakers and advances in racing aerodynamics. The cars were assembled at Lowe's Motor Speedway in May 1998 as part of NASCAR's 50th Anniversary celebration.

Predicting the future is an inexact science at best, but it's fun to speculate on what new technologies the 21st century might hold for stock car racing: Will cars be powered by nuclear energy, or jet engines? Perhaps drivers will use on-board computers to suggest the best line around a track based on chassis setup, remaining fuel and tire wear.

Chances are, those farfetched concepts won't come to pass. In fact, the cars of 2020 or 2040 will closely resemble those we see in NASCAR today. In many respects, the car Dale Jarrett drove to the 1999 NASCAR Winston Cup Series championship was very similar to the Ford David Pearson piloted to the 1969 Series title: Both featured four wheels, a roll cage and hundreds of horsepower in the hands of a skilled driver trying to out duel some 40 other drivers. Of course, the tires and roll cage have seen dramatic improvements through the years, and the engines are much more efficient and powerful.

These changes didn't happen overnight, but evolved a year at a time. Only several decades later can we look back and see how relatively primitive the 1969 Ford is when compared to Jarrett's 1999 Ford Taurus.

(Above) Joe Lee Johnson leads the pack on his way to victory at Nashville in 1959, followed by Johnny Allen (44) and Bob Welborn (49). The cars seem rather quaint, contrasted with the two high-tech cars in the photo at right, which are the products of countless hundreds of hours of testing and design. The Ford Thunderbird on the right was replaced by the Taurus in NASCAR racing at the start of the 1998 season.

*Bobby Labonte's 2000 Pontiac
Grand Prix is the culmination of more than
50 years of stock car engineering, including
advanced aerodynamics, a concept that
would have been completely foreign to stock
car racers in the early years of the sport.*

Richard Petty and Elmo Langley take to the high banks in 1969 race action. Petty's brand new Ford Torino Talladega was designed specifically with racing aerodynamics in mind, and was allowed to compete after a limited number of production models were built for sale to consumers.

No one knows what NASCAR Winston Cup Series cars will look like 25 or 50 years from now. Even 10 years of change can bring incredible advances in this sport.

"It's hard to say what will happen years from now," says Doug Yates, engine builder for the No. 28 Robert Yates Racing team. "If we could be just one year smarter about predicting things now, we'd beat everybody. That's how difficult it is to look even one year down the road."

"Predicting the future in this sport is very difficult," says NASCAR Winston Cup Series Director Gary Nelson. "All we can go by is past history, and go from there — and look at how much the cars have evolved already."

Master engine builder Robert Yates (left) tinkers with one of his high-performance creations. Today's NASCAR Winston Cup Series engines are capable of turning almost 800 horsepower, and turn close to 10,000 rpm.

NASCAR stock cars have made tremendous strides in the half-century since the organization's birth. In the beginning, stock car racing was indeed just that. Men — and a few women — would literally buy cars straight off the showroom floor and race them on the sands of Daytona Beach and at dirt tracks around the country. Hence the aptly named "Strictly Stock" Division, the forerunner of today's NASCAR Winston Cup Series.

Jim Paschal (above) and Cotton Owens (right) with their 1950s racers. Early stock cars were exactly that, stock models often driven right off the showroom floor.

(Left) (From left) Bobby Allison, Tiny Lund and LeeRoy Yarbrough mix it up on the track in this 1960s shot. Tight, hard-fought racing has been an essential element in NASCAR's growth. (Below) The famous winged Dodge Daytona and Plymouth Superbird hit the tracks in 1969 and 1970 as Chrysler's counter to Ford's Torino Talladega. The "special edition" racers were outlawed after 1970, but they had served their purpose of demonstrating the effects of aerodynamics in dramatic fashion, and thus had a profound impact on the evolution of stock cars.

Bobby Allison (No. 15) overtakes Grant Adcox (41) and Dave Marcis (2) at Atlanta in 1978. Through the 1970s, the cars were still modified versions of production models built for the street, using factory frames, body panels, even bumpers.

But as the sport grew, the cars began to evolve, subtly at first, then more and more radically. The quest for safety drove most of these early changes, many of which, with some modifications, remain intact to this day.

Driver safety has always been the paramount concern of NASCAR officials. Safety innovations such as the fresh air system and window net (below) and the roll cage (right) have evolved over the years.

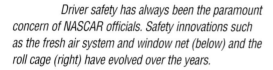

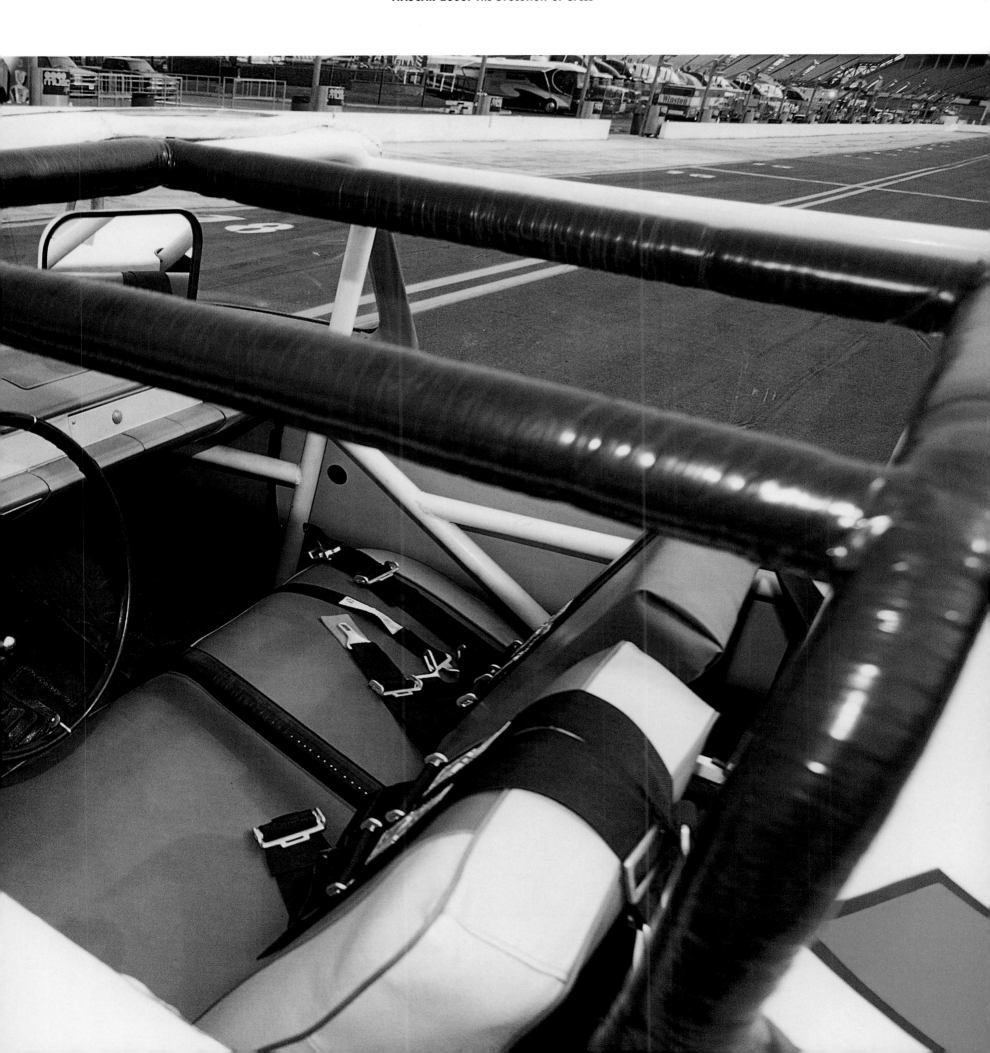

Beginning with the 1960s, a number of major safety innovations were unleashed, including beefed up chassis and roll cage designs; leak-resistant fuel bladders that reduce the risk of fire; and the inner-liner, or a tire within a tire, which helps the driver maintain control after tire failure.

Likewise, safety provided the impetus behind what drivers wore. As recently as the mid-1960s, drivers still competed in races clad in blue jeans and a T-shirt. However, before the decade was out, everyone was wearing fire-retardant driving suits. A similar evolution saw the drivers' headgear change from leather strap-ons in the early days to the impact-resistant, full-faced helmets drivers wear today.

Look for gradual refinement in all driver safety equipment in the coming years. The most likely development is a driver's suit that would protect a driver from fire in all but the worst-case scenarios. Drivers have been the biggest benefactors of many of the technological breakthroughs in recent years, in everything from redesigned seats to roll cage design, all intended to make NASCAR arguably the safest form of motorsports in the world.

Through the years, the cockpit of a NASCAR Winston Cup Series car became stripped of all non-essential items, both for weight, safety and functional reasons. In this old photo, note the shoulder and leg pads, which helped hold the driver in place. The current design (opposite page) is not only safer, but much more comfortable for the driver.

Bill Rexford takes a moment to pose with his car in 1950. Rexford's casual attire — slacks and a T-shirt — were the norm for drivers until the 1960s, when safety concerns led NASCAR to mandate the use of fire resistent uniforms.

Today's race cars are built from the ground up, piece by piece, in accordance to specifications, making the finished product incredibly strong.

Through the years, NASCAR teams and officials have shown great innovation whenever a safety issue arose.

In the mid-1960s, several fiery accidents prompted the development of the fuel bladder (top and opposite page), which surrounds the fuel cell and prevents the spread of fuel in an accident.

After accidents in open-wheel racing in which wheels separated from the cars, NASCAR officials mandated wheel tethers (center), which hold the wheel to the car in the event of an accident.

Dale Jarrett flipped his Ford at Daytona in 1999 (below right), yet the driver walked away unscathed, thanks to one of the earliest, and most effective safety advances, the roll cage.

As long as racers race, accidents will occur.
But the constant development of safety-related devices
has minimized risk.

Ricky Rudd (top) and Rusty Wallace model the latest in racing helmet designs, which bear little resemblance to the headgear worn by Buddy Baker (opposite page) during the 1966 season. Helmets today are lighter and stronger than ever, and further advances in design are inevitable. Likewise, today's footwear does a much better job of protecting drivers than the tennis shoes and loafers favored by drivers in the early years.

An essential element to driver safety is gloves, which protect drivers' hands from the extreme temperatures in and around today's race cars. Most drivers also feel that gloves enhance comfort and control.

Drivers' suits, such as this one worn by Ward Burton are among the most important safety developments made over the years. Made from high-tech, fire resistant fibers, materials and designs are constantly being updated to improve safety and driver comfort. They are also one of the best opportunities to display sponsors' logos.

Even small changes in car designs have had a significant impact on driver safety. Case in point: In the mid-

1990s, after a number of cars became airborne in accidents at high-speed tracks, car owner Jack Roush spearheaded a

movement to introduce roof flaps. The flaps, thin strips of metal that are tucked away into the roofline under

normal circumstances, pop up when the car turns

around, breaking the aerodynamic flow

and typically keeping the car on the ground.

Jack Roush, one of the top car owners in the sport, helped develop these roof flaps in the mid-1990s, in response to the growing problem of cars getting airborne in superspeedway incidents. The flaps remain tucked into the car's roofline under normal conditions, but deploy when a car turns around in an accident, popping up and breaking the aerodynamic flow over the car to help keep it on the ground.

Looking at the high-tech world of NASCAR today brings to mind the infamous words of the U.S. Patents Office director around the end of the 19th century, who noted that there wasn't any need for his department anymore, as all the important inventions had already been developed. (Still to come, of course, were airplanes, TV, radios, rockets, computers, etc.)

It's easy to look at the high-tech world of NASCAR in the year 2000 and have a similar feeling. How can engine builders improve parts that are currently computer-designed with almost microscopic tolerances? And it's hard to imagine making gains in aerodynamics, when a team's engineer can now tweak a fraction of an inch of sheet metal and turn it into an advantage on the track.

Yet race cars will continue to evolve, though in what manner is anyone's guess. Some predictions are a given: Obviously, parts and components will continue to become more durable and more efficient. But foreseeing more fundamental changes in stock cars is much tougher. Will we see cars hitting 250 mph? How about on-board computers making all the critical decisions for the driver? The answer to those questions is an emphatic "no," say those who make their living in the sport.

The fact is, NASCAR does not take full advantage of many sources of technology now available. For example, cars in other racing series have composite bodies, fuel injection and computer telemetry for making adjustments to the car as it circles the track. All of those are strictly forbidden in NASCAR.

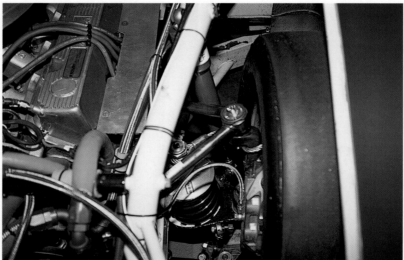

(Top Right) The fresh air circulation system was a significant development in both driver safety and comfort. The continuous flow of fresh, cool air not only protects against drivers breathing gases and fumes, but the cooler air is also very effective in controlling body temperature, which keeps drivers more fresh and comfortable in their race cars, where temperatures commonly reach 140 degrees or more. (Center Right and Bottom Right) Wheel and hood tethers are recent safety improvements mandated by NASCAR to reduce the possibility of parts being separated from the cars during an accident.

Engine development has been ongoing since the first days of NASCAR racing. The contrast between today's powerplants (left) and those of 20 years ago (above) is evident in these photos. Today, a NASCAR Winston Cup Series racing engine is a model of efficiency. Engine builders, using high-performance parts, have developed incredible gains in horsepower in recent years. Is there a limit to how much power a NASCAR racing engine can produce? Obviously, yes, but engine builders have not reached that peak yet.

A new concept that came into the picture some 10 years ago was the use of testing and wind tunnels (the technique to measure how air travels over a race-ready car body). Each can be a huge cost to the team owner, but has made the difference between winning and losing on many occasions.

"I think the technology is such that you see more and more stuff when you go test now," Buddy Parrott says. "NASCAR won't let us have on-board computers at the race track, but during our seven tests, we have to do that.

"The wind tunnel time helps us get the bodies right. Ford's technology group, Chevrolet's technology group, Pontiac — you know, everybody is working to make the ultimate race car. NASCAR has got the biggest job in the whole deal: to make sure that all the cars are on an equal playing field to provide the best and most exciting competition for the fans."

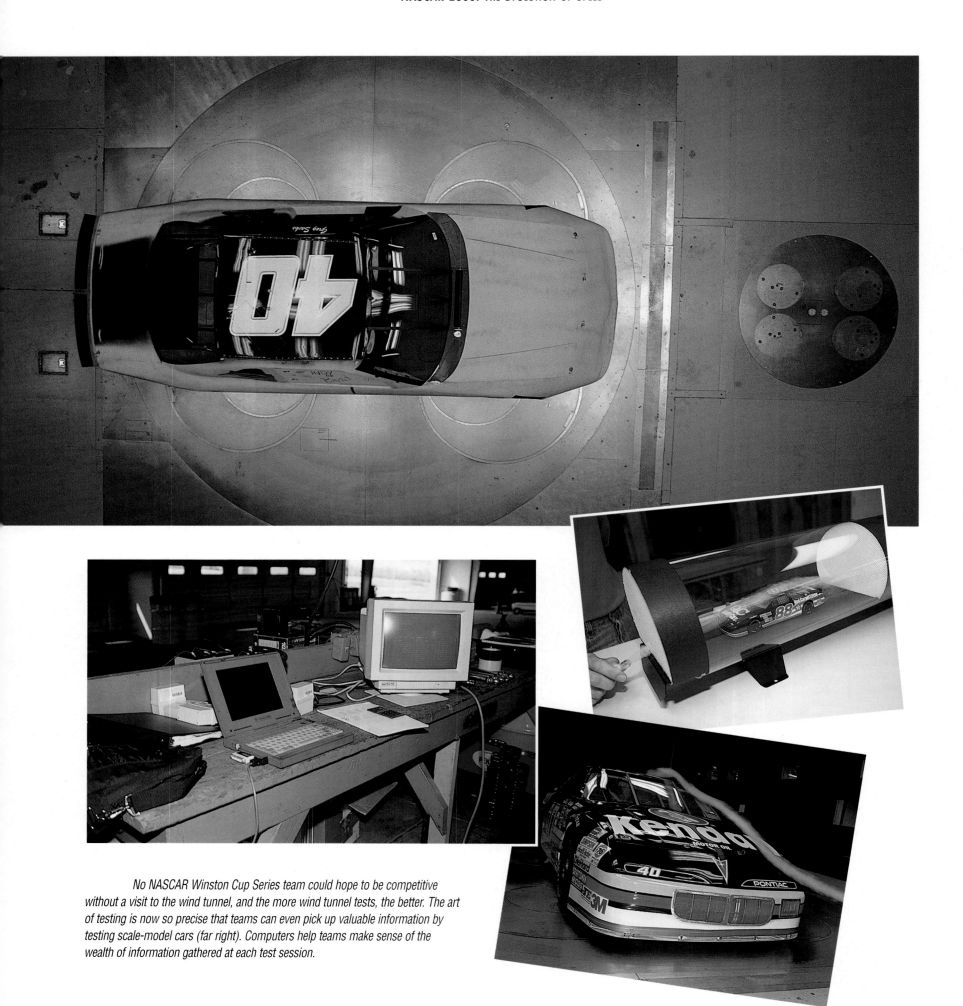

No NASCAR Winston Cup Series team could hope to be competitive without a visit to the wind tunnel, and the more wind tunnel tests, the better. The art of testing is now so precise that teams can even pick up valuable information by testing scale-model cars (far right). Computers help teams make sense of the wealth of information gathered at each test session.

Top speeds for NASCAR Winston Cup Series cars have actually fallen during the past few years. Bill Elliott set the all-time NASCAR qualifying record with a lap at almost 213 mph at Talladega in 1987. Almost 15 years later, no one comes close to approaching that speed. Why? In the late 1980s, NASCAR instituted carburetor restrictor plates to slow cars down at the two fastest tracks, Talladega and Daytona. Those plates limit speeds to the 190-200 mph range.

"I think we'd be in the mid-220 mph range now, if you had left all the rules the same and there were no restrictor plates, and no restriction on the spoiler angle," says Larry McReynolds, crew chief for Richard Childress Racing and driver Mike Skinner.

Bill Elliott leads the field in 1980s action at Michigan International Speedway. Elliott set the all-time NASCAR speed record with a qualifying lap of more than 212 mph at Talladega. Speeds at the circuit's fastest tracks have fallen since the institution of restrictor plates in the late 1980s.

Gary Nelson does not apologize for NASCAR's somewhat low-tech approach, explaining there are several reasons for that philosophy. There are safety considerations, of course, not to mention the quest to ensure parity. But behind it all is the no-frills, down-to-earth philosophy of driver versus driver, which has been a staple of NASCAR racing from the beginning.

"If you look at it, we've got a carburetor, which is pretty much antiquated," says Nelson. "We've got a lot of steel and metal in our race cars, while other forms of racing have on-board computers, processors, high-tech composite frames and bodies, and other components on the car that make a lot of their sport technician versus technician."

Drivers, team owners and most everyone else in the sport unanimously agree on one thing — faster speeds do not necessarily equate to progress. More importantly, they don't mean a better show for the fans.

"I don't think NASCAR is about speed," says Doug Yates. "I think NASCAR is about a good, competitive race, whether we're going 215 or 180 mph."

In lieu of faster speeds, what can fans expect, say, in the year 2025? As with the roof flaps example, changes will be subtle, but will enhance performance and/or safety.

"Everything will continue to improve," says McReynolds. "Gains in aerodynamics will improve, you'll see changes in the chassis. I can't say — and no one can say — what those changes will be, but I think you'll continue to see a gradual refinement of what we're doing today."

"It's kind of scary what they could do. The aerodynamics of cars will be incredible," says Tim Beverley, owner of Tyler Jet Motorsports. "You look at what they could do right now at the restrictor-plate races. Without those plates, right now we could be going 230 mph. That could happen given the aerodynamics.

"But give NASCAR all the credit for always acting in the interest of safety first. If they can run those speeds safely, they will. But none of us wants to risk a major accident."

Teams go through preseason testing at Daytona International Speedway before the 2000 season. During each test session, teams look for any advantage, however small, they can find. That's the nature of evolution in stock car racing — progress is usually measured not in leaps and bounds, but fractions of a second.

A number of aerodynamic and other advances will emerge from Detroit. NASCAR's booming popularity is due in large part to the fact that fans can identify with the cars on the track, which look similar to the cars they can buy at their local dealership. In that respect, the thousands of engineers who tweak and redesign passenger cars on an annual basis ensure NASCAR's evolution.

And in turn, the experience the manufacturers glean from NASCAR is invaluable. Doug Duchardt, the General Motors group manager for oval track racing, says the technology that propels NASCAR winners today will be found in the passenger cars of tomorrow.

"For GM, we've made a large investment in push-rod engines for the future," Duchardt says. "They are in our Corvettes, Camaros and passenger trucks. NASCAR is a great avenue to test the limits of these engines."

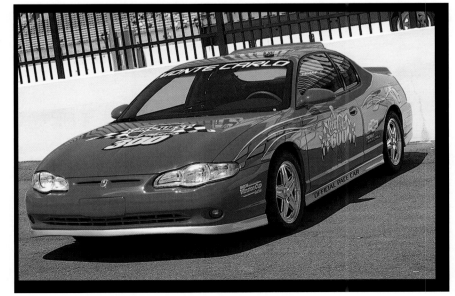

Engineers with the automakers will continue to play their part in the evolution of NASCAR, as they did with the introduction of the Ford Taurus in the late 1990s (above, flanked by the racing versions of Jeremy Mayfield on the left and Rusty Wallace). Chevrolet's retooled Monte Carlo (left), prompted changes to its NASCAR brethren.

While NASCAR will help extend the bounds of passenger car technology well into the 21st century, the sport itself will see radical changes of its own in the garage area and in the shop.

One of the more interesting innovations will be the aforementioned driver simulator. Extremely primitive versions of this can already be found at "NASCAR Silicon Motor Speedways" around the country, where fans can run virtual laps at a simulated NASCAR Winston Cup Series track.

Future versions of this software will be much more realistic, allowing a driver to use the simulator to prepare for races.

"It's no different than a flight simulator," says McReynolds. "That's definitely a possibility. That would be a tremendous help for rookies going into a new track, showing them the line you run, the banking, the tire wear. Will it include every variable? No. But it will give the driver a great idea of what to expect."

In the early days of NASCAR, mechanics did most of their work in tiny garages, or even under the proverbial shade tree. Today's race shops are a marvel of modern technology, with millions of dollars worth of high-tech equipment available to help engineers perform their jobs.

Likewise, other computer programs will help engine builders, shock technicians and others run a simulated race, just to check out the performance of their specific components.

"I think what we're going to see is a computer program to help predict what the engine goes through at the track in a 500-mile race, and have it so when that engine leaves the shop, it's ready to go in the race car with no adjustments," says Yates, who points out that first-generation virtual engine simulators are already available.

In the past decade, faster, more powerful computers have radically changed the way we live, helping us surf the Internet, e-mail friends and do some of our shopping at home.

Although it has not embraced computer technology as much as other forms of racing, NASCAR has not been immune to the influence of the technology. NASCAR Winston Cup Series teams now use powerful computers during test sessions to analyze scores of variables.

Rules designed to maintain parity among competitors have consistently resulted in close, exciting race action such as this, and NASCAR has demonstrated its intention to maintain this concept by changing the rules as technology fuels the evolution of machines.

While NASCAR has frowned on the use of on-board computers during races, Gary Nelson says the Series will continue to allow use of the most powerful, sophisticated computer in the world: the human brain.

"NASCAR has always taken a low-tech approach," says Nelson. "We don't really embrace high-tech computers or processors, largely because we've always been a driver's series. We think the driver should compete against the other driver with cars as close as we can make them by the rules.

"We're not really that excited about on-board processors that make decisions to help the driver. When you think of our basic philosophy — driver versus driver — the processor is really behind the driver's ears, and his sensors are the seat of his pants and his feet on the pedals."

Yet computer technology will play an increasingly important role in everything from test sessions, to building engines, shocks and chassis. Almost every race team now uses computers during testing, and as computing power has expanded almost exponentially, the telemetry units are now capable of measuring hundreds of different variables.

"We've got systems right now where we can totally generate what the car's going to do on the computer," says Beverley. "How will that change in the future? Look at it this way: Four, five years ago, who was using the Internet? Now, people are wearing it out. I think it will be real interesting to see in the next few years what happens."

(Above) While the use of computers is severely limited in competition, they are absolutely essential in test sessions. Telemetry generated from the car during testing is analyzed using sophisticated software, and what is learned is employed during the race. (Left) Modern-day race cars are hand crafted by highly-specialized technicians, but are still relatively free of sophisticated electronic devices and expensive, space-age materials.

Other advances in technology will be greeted with open arms by drivers. Imagine a day when drivers will motor around a speedway with their cockpit temperature a cool 72 degrees. Sounds impossible, considering the temperature in some cars has been measured at close to 200 degrees. Advances in insulation and cooling technology will one day help keep the engine and exhaust heat in the engine compartment, where it belongs.

So while the future has yet to be written, McReynolds says we will continue to be astounded as NASCAR progresses through the new century.

(Top) The special challenges encountered on road courses have fueled specific developments, including high-tech transmissions that do not require pressing the clutch during rigorous shifting. (Above) What will race cars be like in the future? One can only speculate. But it is certain that the development of NASCAR Winston Cup Series cars will continue, and will remain an important and exciting aspect in the evolution of the sport.

PALACES

OF

SPEED

It's every promoter's dream — and we're not talking about a three-way fight to the finish, either. Instead, it's the chance to build a race track from scratch. With an unlimited budget, no less.

Construction is in full swing at the new Kentucky Speedway in August of 1999.

In recent years, tracks have sprouted in Las Vegas, Fontana, Calif., and Forth Worth, Texas. And while the budgets may not have been completely unlimited, the painstaking planning has resulted in some true palaces of speed.

Are such examples simply the beginning of even more remarkable things to come, or has track building reached a peak? It's a question that will be answered over time, but some of the sport's leading minds believe the best is yet to come.

They see future technological advances taking fans to new plateaus in terms of the entertainment experience. But in what may truly be a case of going back to the future, some of the tracks may bear more than a passing resemblance to the facilities that helped NASCAR get its start.

And while no one expects to be racing on a beach any time soon, or on a three-tenths of a mile dirt bullring, it seems clear that the sport's roots will remain firmly entrenched in the new millennium.

(Below Left) The California Speedway sign just outside of the main entrance officially announces the track was ready for business in this 1997 photo. (Below) Fans begin to fill the stands at California to see the action on the track and to follow their favorite driver on the electronic scoring pylon. (Right) Jeff Gordon (24) leads the field down pit road during a caution in the inaugural event at California Speedway in 1997. Gordon went on to win in his home state.

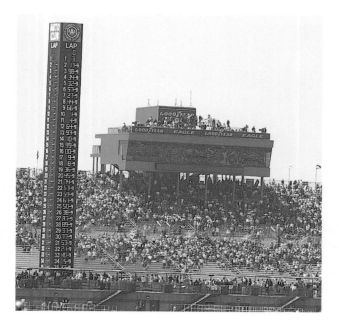

(Above) The finishing touches are put on Texas Motor Speedway early in 1997 in preparation for its addition to the NASCAR Winston Cup Series schedule. (Left) Dale Jarrett (88) leads Jeff Gordon (24) in front of a packed crowd at Texas Motor Speedway's inaugural NASCAR Winston Cup Series event held April 6, 1997.

A sea of campers fill the infield at Las Vegas Motor Speedway in 1997 (Inset) Light shines brightly over the track as well as the city of Las Vegas

Ask Humpy Wheeler, one of the most imaginative track promoters NASCAR has ever known. Lowe's Motor Speedway may not be the newest track going, but with luxury suites and condo- miniums galore, you'd never know it. The 1.5-mile layout has been a design that's been emulated at other facilities.

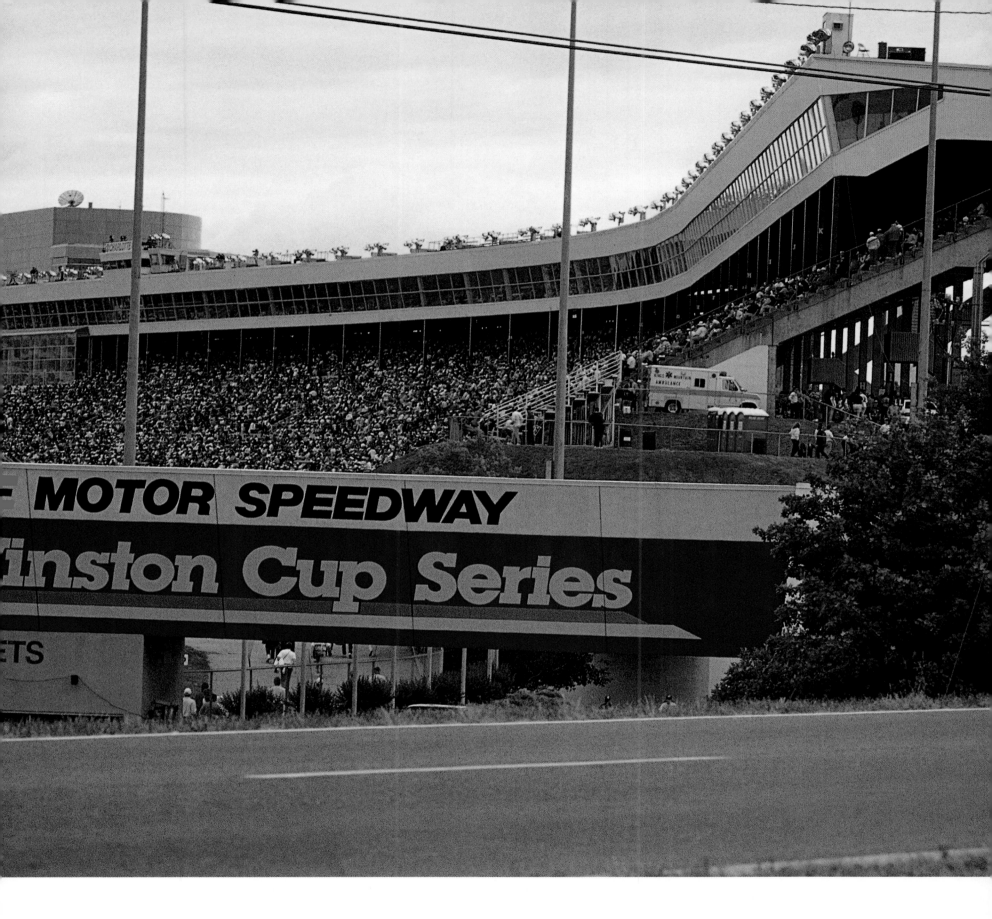

(Right) Lowe's Motor Speedway (formerly named Charlotte Motor Speedway) is one of the great showplaces on the NASCAR Winston Cup Series schedule, and it is packed to capacity each time NASCAR visits there. (Inset) The Speedway Club overlooks the track and features dining on white linen and china.

The Speedway Club at Texas Motor
Speedway (right and opposite page) also gives one
a good look at the action from high above the
track. (Below Right) Mark Maudlin of Petty
Enterprises puts the workout room at California
Speedway to good use.

The mirrored glass that covers the media center at Homestead-Miami Speedway reflects the track, the cars and fans on the frontstretch area in front of it.

Now, though, Wheeler has a grandiose vision of what he'd like to see built next.

"It would probably be a three-quarter mile Bristol," says Wheeler, encompassing the length of Richmond International Raceway with the high banks of the Tennessee oval's half mile. "I would have the garage area — which Bristol doesn't really have — underneath the track, underneath the infield.

"By that time, there will be enough dollars in this sport to where you could do that. Just build a big basement. Then you'd drive the cars right out of it. That would leave the infield beautiful green grass, just gorgeously landscaped. You wouldn't have any high bushes, but azaleas. It would be a beautiful area. You'd also have the pits."

The high-banked short track called Bristol Motor Speedway is the place where some of the most incredible action of the season takes place twice each year. The intimate half-mile seats more than 130,000 fans.

That folks, is just the beginning of Wheeler's ideal playground, one that would appeal to drivers and fans alike. Richmond's layout traditionally leads to great racing, a trait that results as well from Bristol's steep banks. And with more than 100,000 fans attending races at both venues, it's a given that smaller tracks can still handle ever-growing crowds.

(Above) Ken Schrader leads the field up to speed at the 0.75-mile Richmond (Va.) International Raceway in this 1993 photo. (Left) Dave Marcis (71) leads J.D. McDuffie and D.K. Ulrich during a caution on the old Richmond Fairgrounds track in the early 1980s. Leaders Darrell Waltrip (88) and Richard Petty (43) pit for fuel. The track was reconstructed and lengthened to its current D-oval configuration during the summer of 1988 between NASCAR Winston Cup Series events held there that year.

A very restless short-track field works to get around the near-flat turns of Martinsville (Va.) Speedway in 1998. Fans can see the action from any seat in the house at the pristine half-mile oval.

(Right) Terry Labonte
finds the point at North Wilkesboro,
N.C., in April of 1996. (Below)
Mark Martin (6) shows his colors
from the front at North Carolina
Motor Speedway (now called North
Carolina Speedway) in
Rockingham, N.C., early in the
1997 season.

Fans will be able to attend races at this future venue knowing they won't have to play hooky from work the next day, either. Rainouts will be a thing of the past, something that will make things better for drivers, crewmen and fans alike.

In some respects, tracks may resemble Texas Stadium, home of the Dallas Cowboys.

"I would have it partially domed," he said. "I would have the grandstands, the track and pit road covered. Then I would have a huge hole (in the middle). I would do that with synthetic material that's available today that's tensioned with cables — so we'd be able to run the race in any kind of weather.

"Being more than half outdoors, you wouldn't have a ventilation problem, either. Hot air rises and that's what a race car's exhaust is."

Such a facility sounds about perfect once fans reach the track. But in case getting there truly is half the fun, one of Wheeler's contemporaries has got that idea covered. Atlanta Motor Speedway President Ed Clark believes transportation issues will be one of the biggest improvements as time goes by.

Instead of sitting in lines of traffic, Clark sees fans' trips to the tracks running smoothly, leaving them more time to enjoy the amenities the tracks will present fans both young and old.

"Not only will tracks be located next to a major highway, but you'll be located next to an airport and there will probably be some other form of public transportation where there will be a major dedicated bus route or perhaps a rail line," Clark said. "It will be much more than a couple driving in their car to an event.

"There will be a dedicated roadway or tramway encircling the facility where people can be dropped off at the gate closest to the section they are in. And I think you'll continue to see the camping part of it grow, there will be more and better amenities for them as well."

Traffic is heavy as fans file out of Talladega Superspeedway after a NASCAR Winston Cup Series event in 1999. It doesn't really matter what is driven to the race track, as the variety of vehicles shows.

Rusty Wallace stands in front of his fleet of airplanes that take him to NASCAR Winston Cup Series events, as well as to many personal appearances for his fans and his business obligations.

The playground at Talladega Superspeedway is always filled with the children of many of the NASCAR Winston Cup Series and NASCAR Busch Series, Grand National Division drivers. Playgrounds like this one allow competitors and their wives to tend to necessary activities at the track, while knowing their children are safe and having fun.

A few race fans stand in the center

walkway and check out the garage area at

California Speedway as crewmembers continue

their work in the garage stalls.

(Opposite page) A city is made of sponsors' hospitality tents just outside the fourth turn at Dover Downs International Speedway. (Left) Bill Elliott's Ford sits ready for fan inspection at Bristol Motor Speedway in August of 1999. (Below) Souvenir vendors sell their wares among flags and cardboard stand-ups that help make up the attractions of a NASCAR Winston Cup Series event.

Greg Penske, a senior vice president at International Speedway Corporation, envisions tracks operating more like football and baseball stadiums with in-seat service, food courts and sports bars. But the biggest changes will be to the infields.

"Each motorhome spot could have a pedestal with a television hook-up, Internet access and the ability to order food or merchandise delivered right to your door," Penske said. "You could tap into concerts or drive-in movies right at your site.

"One of the great things about NASCAR is that we have our fans at the event for three or four days. I see infields turning into small cities, where people don't need to leave the track for any reason."

Driver Rick Mast hasn't contemplated things of that nature, but he agrees it will be important for fans to have easy access to the track.

"I see these big monorails or trams shuttling people in and out," he said. "I see probably everything lit, with us running prime-time races on television with more races and shorter races for TV."

(Left) Jeff Gordon (24) leads Geoffrey Bodine (7), Dale Earnhardt (3) and Bobby Labonte (22) in the Inaugural Brickyard 400 at Indianapolis Motor Speedway in 1994. Gordon went on to victory lane later in the day. (Top) Dover Downs International Speedway is great for both auto racing as well as horse racing, which takes place on the smaller oval surrounded by Dover's one-mile, high-banked concrete surface. (Above) Drivers and team owners enjoy being home — away from home — thanks to some very elegant motor coaches they park close to the garage area.

In the future, fans won't have to wait in line to buy tickets, either — at least not if Wheeler's vision is realized.

"You'd have bought the tickets through that-day's version of the Internet, which will be a big-screen TV," he said. "That TV would be able to see you as well as you see it. Instead of a credit card, I would use the iris of my eye. I would go to the track and each gate would have all that programmed in. I would just look into it and I would gain admission that way. I would also have bought my airline ticket to get to the track that way."

Drivers, mind you, aren't worried about extremely complex issues. All they ask for is a fun place to work. And while there's plenty to be said about high-speed layouts, a number of drivers would love to see more tracks with the characteristics of Bristol and Richmond.

"It wouldn't be a bad thing, it really wouldn't," Dale Jarrett said. "I'd love to see more race tracks like Bristol and Richmond. I think that would be really good. I think we could really have fun.

"I think it would be nice to have a few more three-quarter mile tracks. Very seldom do we go to Richmond and not have a good race. So if they want a mile-and-a-half track, they ought to build two of them."

Bristol Motor Speedway, located in the hills of eastern Tennessee, is one of those fan friendly tracks, as seeing the action is not difficult from virtually anywhere in the stands.

Tony Stewart has run virtually every type of car imaginable and agrees that adding a few short tracks would be wonderful.

"Everybody's building great facilities, but it would be nice to see someone build a smaller track that could hold the same amount of people like they do at Bristol," Stewart said.

Given time, Stewart may well get his wish.

"I think people are going to look for things that are unique," believes Darlington Raceway President Jim Hunter. "There may be another Darlington in the future, where the turns in one end are different from the turns in the other end." Michael Waltrip thinks Hunter and others looking to recapture the past in the tracks of the future have the right idea.

"I would have them start building some tracks with banks and maybe characteristics like Darlington or Charlotte," Waltrip said. "Hopefully they'll build tracks with great amenities for the fans around tracks that are somewhat like the ones from the old days.

(Above) Mark Martin travels around the 0.533-mile Bristol track early in the day when the stands are not yet full. (Left) The Inaugural Southern 500 in 1950 at Darlington (S.C.) Raceway was a sight, as the field was lined up three-wide at the start of NASCAR's first superspeedway event.

"Richmond is great, Bristol's great. Martinsville certainly has a place for us. Darlington and Rockingham are also great tracks."

In a way, many involved in the sport see NASCAR embarking on the era currently gripping baseball. Three decades ago, city after city built stadiums that were symmetrical, with the outfield dimensions the same from place to place. But once Baltimore built Oriole Park at Camden Yards, the ultimate throwback, people began experimenting. If there are ways to refine the layouts originated at Darlington, Richmond or Martinsville, the drivers would welcome the challenge.

"Richmond produces some very exciting racing, as small as it is," driver Ted Musgrave said.

A huge full moon rises above Lowe's Motor Speedway when it was called Charlotte Motor Speedway in this 1992 photo. At the time, the 1.5-mile facility was the largest lighted sports venue in the world.

(Above) Harry Gant (33) gets some last minute help from a crewmember just before the start of The Winston, a special non-points, all-star event at Charlotte in 1993. (Right) NASCAR Busch Series, Grand National Division driver Todd Bodine, from nearby Chemung, N.Y., hustles through the turns during a NASCAR Winston Cup Series event at Watkins Glen International in 1997.

While the drivers want layouts that will keep them on their toes, they'd also welcome tracks with enhanced safety features. Walls are an area that future improvements will focus on.

"We all have to strive for that," Ed Clark said. "The difficult part is coming up with something that will do the job, soften the blow, but it won't be torn up and have to be replaced every time it's hit. I think if they keep working on it, in the next 10 years — hopefully sooner — somebody's going to come up with an impact barrier that will spring back to its original shape, absorb the impact and not be something that a jagged piece of sheet metal can rip or tear."

(Above Right) New seats are being built around Charlotte in April of 1998, in the track's seemingly never-ending growth. (Below Right) The sign painted on the wall at Bristol Motor Speedway indicates the track owner's plan to add quite a few more seats there, also.

Wheeler and Clark both see major advances in the track surfaces, with Wheeler seeing new synthetic substances replacing rock in the asphalt mixes. That will make the pavement smoother, and longer lasting. He sees the pavement being more like smooth concrete, but with characteristics that allow for plenty of cohesion for the tires.

"It will be something that will give maximum tire wear and will have adhesion that won't change a lot year in and year out," Clark said. "Asphalt, as it gets older, changes quite a bit. Some of the tracks in the sandier areas, when they repave those tracks the surface goes away a lot quicker. But I think there will be polymers that will allow a track to stay consistent for 15 years.

"Then they won't have to come up with a new tire compound every two years because the track's changed."

While safety will be an over-riding concern in the future, the comfort of the fans will be a close second. Wheeler says his dream track will cater to them in a number of ways.

"The seats will be air-conforming seats to your body," he

A look through the sliding glass doors from one of the condominiums at Tara Place at Atlanta Motor Speedway produces a great place from which to watch all the action.

said. "And I think the seats will be a little wider than you have today."

Wheeler believes the seating in the luxury boxes will have interactive capabilities built into each seat. As for the fans in the grandstands, they'll bring with them coin-thin TVs that will be computerized, allowing them to call up statistics and replays at the click of a button.

Those advancements may seem radical, but 20 years ago no one would have imagined condominiums at a race track, so it's obvious that anything is possible with a little bit of vision.

This artist's drawing indicates the future growth of Atlanta Motor Speedway in the years ahead. Note the major traffic arteries and transit systems that will make getting to the track much easier and less time consuming.

"One thing that I see as a possibility is tracks running in and out of a stadium, combining the benefits of the infield with the excitement outside the track, giving more people the ability to be part of the show," Wheeler imagines.

Bristol Motor Speedway General Manager Jeff Byrd has even bigger goals. He'd like to multiply his track. But the clone wouldn't be in another state, it would be right next door.

"Our idea is to create an identical half-mile track right next to the current track at Bristol," Byrd said. "Then we create a tunnel connecting the two tracks and the drivers use both tracks during the race. Instead of 150,000 people seeing the race, we'd have 300,000 seats. Maybe then we could fill all the requests for tickets."

(Above) Pikes Peak International Raceway near Denver, Colorado, entertains some of NASCAR's finest machines when the NASCAR Busch Series and NASCAR Craftsman Truck Series make their annual visits to the spectacular new facility. (Opposite page above) NASCAR Busch Series, Grand National Division action is fierce at Gateway International Raceway in St. Louis in this 1997 photo. (Opposite page below) Pole-winner Ernie Irvan (28) and Robert Yates Racing teammate Dale Jarrett (88) lead the field at Talladega Superspeedway – NASCAR's largest and fastest track – in April of 1996. Sterling Marlin was the eventual race winner.

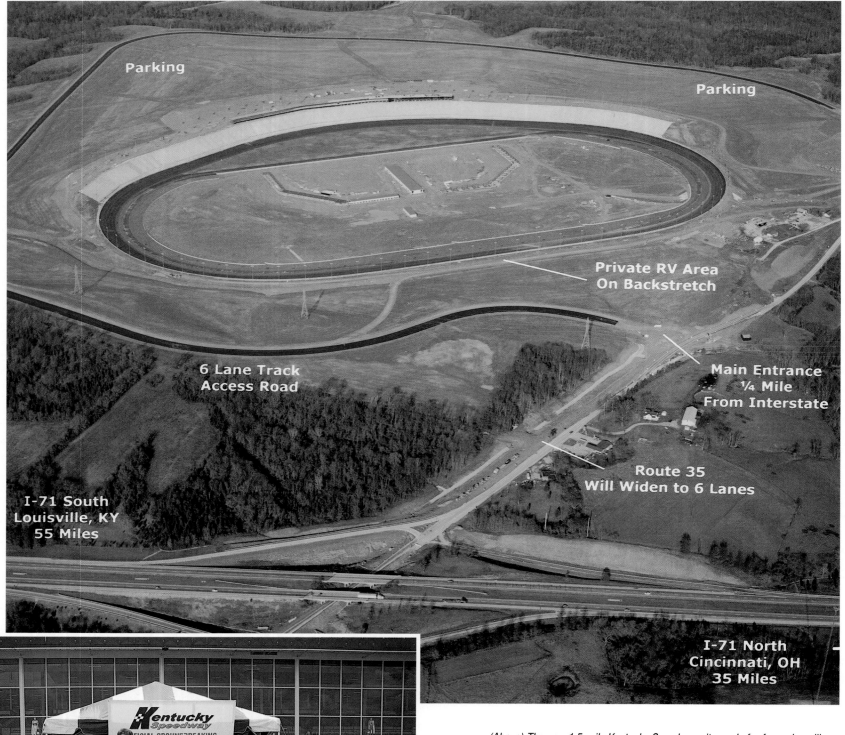

Parking

Parking

Private RV Area
On Backstretch

6 Lane Track
Access Road

Main Entrance
¼ Mile
From Interstate

Route 35
Will Widen to 6 Lanes

I-71 South
Louisville, KY
55 Miles

I-71 North
Cincinnati, OH
35 Miles

(Above) The new 1.5-mile Kentucky Speedway sits ready for fans who will come from the easy access highways close by. (Left) Kentucky natives Darrell Waltrip (on podium at left) and Jeremy Mayfield (podium, right) participate in the ground-breaking ceremony at Kentucky Speedway in July 1998. Joining them are former and current NASCAR drivers (with shovels from left) Harry Gant, Geoffrey Bodine and Cale Yarborough, along with (from right) Ken Schrader, Buddy Baker, Kenny Wallace and David Pearson. (Opposite page) Fans pack the huge frontstretch grandstand for another NASCAR event at the famed triangular Pocono Raceway in northeast Pennsylvania. The track's unique layout gives the superspeedway a personality all its own.

But for every new-fangled facility, the NASCAR of the future will still have a few homey facilities reminiscent of the good old days. As baseball has Fenway Park and Wrigley Field, there will always be places like Pocono Raceway.

Located in the Pocono Mountains, the Mattioli family makes everyone feel like they're at home. And no matter how much other venues may change, Dr. Joseph Mattioli aims to keep things that way. Sure the track will have all the necessary amenities, but part of its charm will be that it will never forget its roots.

"If I built a track again, I would still go with the configuration we have," Mattioli said of the unique tri-oval. "The grandstands, the thing that we sell the most of — the tickets that go first — are the club seats. We would build more of those.

"And we'll have the place manicured, with lots of trees and shrubs. It will be all paved and clean."

Clark's Atlanta facility has condos and other wonderful things, but he supports Mattioli's way of thinking.

"One of the things that has helped build the sport is the diversity in the type of areas we have," Clark said. "You have people in the infield who wouldn't be caught dead in a suite, you've got people in the suites who wouldn't care to go to the infield, and people sitting in the stands who wouldn't care for one of the other choices. I think you're probably going to see more diversity along those lines. And better service to the customers."

More importantly, Mattioli hit on the issue that every track in the future will have to concern itself with. Whether it's a facility with an underground garage, condominiums and sky boxes galore, or a road course in Northern California, there's one thing they'll all have in common.

"We're going to eliminate waiting in line to use the bathroom," Mattioli said. "You have to have an overabundance in that department."

The signs around the newly constructed Kansas City Speedway show the community's anticipation of the scheduled opening for the 2001 season.

There's one more thing that won't change come 2020 or 2098, when NASCAR's celebrating a century of excellence.

"The one thing that will never change, no matter what goes on at the facilities themselves, is that when they drop the green flag, the sport is still the same sport," Mattioli says. "That's the neat thing about our sport right now. When they drop the green flag, to me it's just like it was when I was 16 years old and starting my first race on dirt."

It's just that now, the grandstands and other facilities are a whole lot nicer.

Dale Earnhardt (3) and Loy Allen (19) lead the way in Daytona's 400-mile event in July 1994. Daytona International Speedway – "The Birthplace of Speed" – remains as NASCAR's premier venue.

FANS AND TECHNOLOGY

(ABOVE) A SMALL CAMERA SITS READY TO BE INSTALLED INSIDE A RACE CAR TO HELP BRING THE SPORT CLOSER TO THE FANS WATCHING ON TELEVISION. OVER THE PAST

20 YEARS, IN-CAR CAMERAS HAVE BECOME MUCH MORE VERSATILE THAN THE ORIGINAL HEAVIER MODELS. (LEFT) WARD BURTON, ONE OF THE MOST PERSONABLE

DRIVERS IN THE SPORT, SIGNS AUTOGRAPHS FOR HIS FANS AT MICHIGAN SPEEDWAY DURING THE 1995 NASCAR WINSTON CUP SERIES SEASON.

NASCAR 2000 marks the beginning of a dazzling technological journey that will see fans experience NASCAR Winston Cup Series, NASCAR Busch Series and NASCAR Craftsman Truck Series races with a realism and intensity that was inconceivable even a few short years ago.

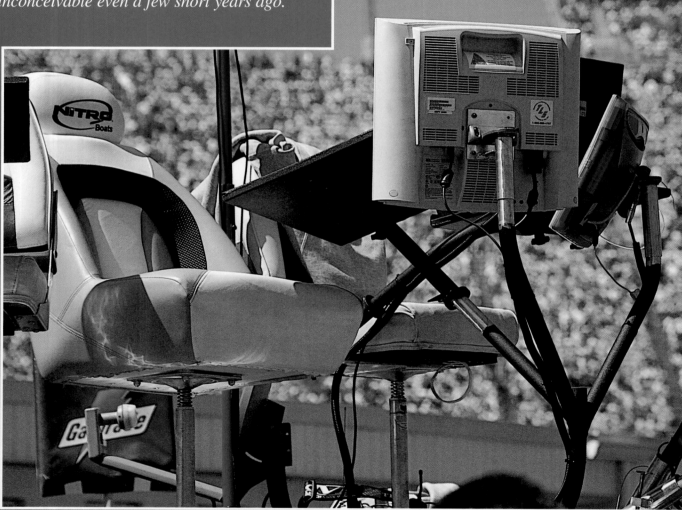

(Top Left) A camera is mounted where fans at home can get a much closer look at pit stops on pit road. (Below Left) A scanner featuring radio transmissions between drivers and teams is being programmed with the proper frequencies. Popular among fans, scanners give their listeners added insight to the action on the track. (Above) Atop what is known as a "war wagon" or rolling tool cart taken to pit road, computer screens allow teams to track their drivers' progress more easily during a race.

Virtual reality is the hot ticket these days, allowing fans to get right inside the cars with the drivers through special electronic technology.

Starting with the 2001 season, the way fans at home and in the grandstands experience the thrill of NASCAR racing will be profoundly and permanently enhanced and expanded.

Over the course of the next few seasons, fans will have a plethora of new options and ways to follow races, from simply tuning in on their televisions like they always have, to viewing an entire race from the in-car camera of their favorite driver while listening to that team's scanner and monitoring real-time scoring live on the Internet.

The fans are the foundation of NASCAR's success in the year 2000. Week after week, wearing the souvenir clothing of their favorite drivers and teams, they turn out in force. They are considered by those in the business as the most loyal of any professional sport.

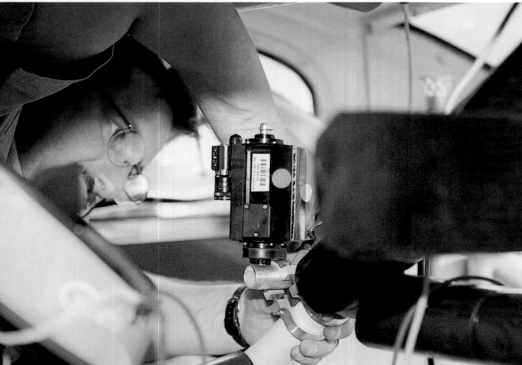

(Top) Fans display all types of flags atop their respective motorhomes from the infield at a NASCAR Winston Cup Series event. (Above) A television technician installs an in-car camera by clamping the unit to one of the rear support bars — part of a race car's roll cage. (Right) A camera is directed back toward the rear of a NASCAR Busch Series car to pick up other competitors as they drop to the inside of the track.

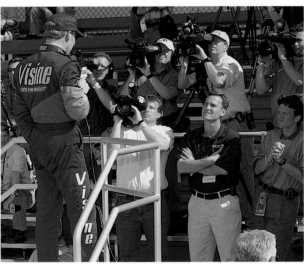

(Far Left) A computer technician checks data concerning a variety of vital points dealing with a race car's setup. Computers can be used during test sessions, but not during any given NASCAR Winston Cup Series event weekend. (Left) NASCAR driver Matt Kenseth answers questions and poses for television cameras after his NASCAR Busch Series, Grand National Division victory at Daytona in February 2000. (Right) The action in the NASCAR Busch Series, Grand National Division can be just as competitive as what is seen among the NASCAR Winston Cup Series regulars. Sponsorships are also gaining momentum in that division as far as the larger, more recognizable brand names among the general public.

New broadcast technologies will offer advanced real-time telemetry and the ability to isolate individual cars with spot shadows and "glow clouds." Detailed statistical information on every driver, team and track will be at fans' fingertips as television and computer technologies converge.

Fans will be able to watch virtually every moment of a race weekend on television, from the time the haulers roll onto the track, through practice, qualifying, driver meetings, chapel service and, of course, the race itself. You'll even be able to hang around and watch cars being torn down and inspected in tech after the race.

In short, thanks to NASCAR 2000, race fans are about to discover a whole new world of options that they didn't even know existed.

Team transporters are rolling race shops, having an extra car on the rack up top and enough parts on board to rebuild virtually any portion of the race car. They also act as great areas for sponsor promotion when traveling up and down the highway.

The Television Contract

On Nov. 9, 1999, officials from NASCAR, NBC, Fox and Turner
Broadcasting met in New York's Four Seasons Hotel to reach final terms on a landmark
six-year television contract. The deal firmly established NASCAR as a major player in the
sporting world, alongside the National Football League, Major League Baseball and the
National Basketball Association.

The breadth and impact of the deal will change the sport forever.

In 2001, Fox Sports and its FX cable network will broadcast every NASCAR
Winston Cup Series and NASCAR Busch Series, Grand National Division race during the first
half of the season, while races in the second half of the year will be split between NBC Sports
and TBS Superstation.

Fans will benefit from the new deal in a number of ways. First and foremost,
fully 70 percent of the NASCAR Winston Cup Series races will be carried on broadcast television and 30 percent on cable, instead of the other way around.

NASCAR's new television partners will be able to make significant investments in
new technologies and promotion to enhance the viewing experience for fans.

Races will be easier to find for fans, since fewer channels will be carrying them,
and both pre- and post-race coverage will be profoundly enhanced.

(Opposing Page) Getting the
action while it's transpiring at speeds nearing
200 miles per hour takes the steady hand of
an experienced cameraman. (Above Right)
Television announcer Mike Massaro prepares
to talk with Matt Kenseth in the garage at
Homestead-Miami Speedway.

Electronic signage is put into place at each of the 34 races on the annual schedule as well as any special non-points events held each year to spell out what's really going on for the fans in attendance. Also, an army of mobile television units can be seen each week on both the NASCAR Winston Cup Series and NASCAR Busch Series circuits. The sport of stock car racing is now considered as professional as the traditional stick-and-ball sports.

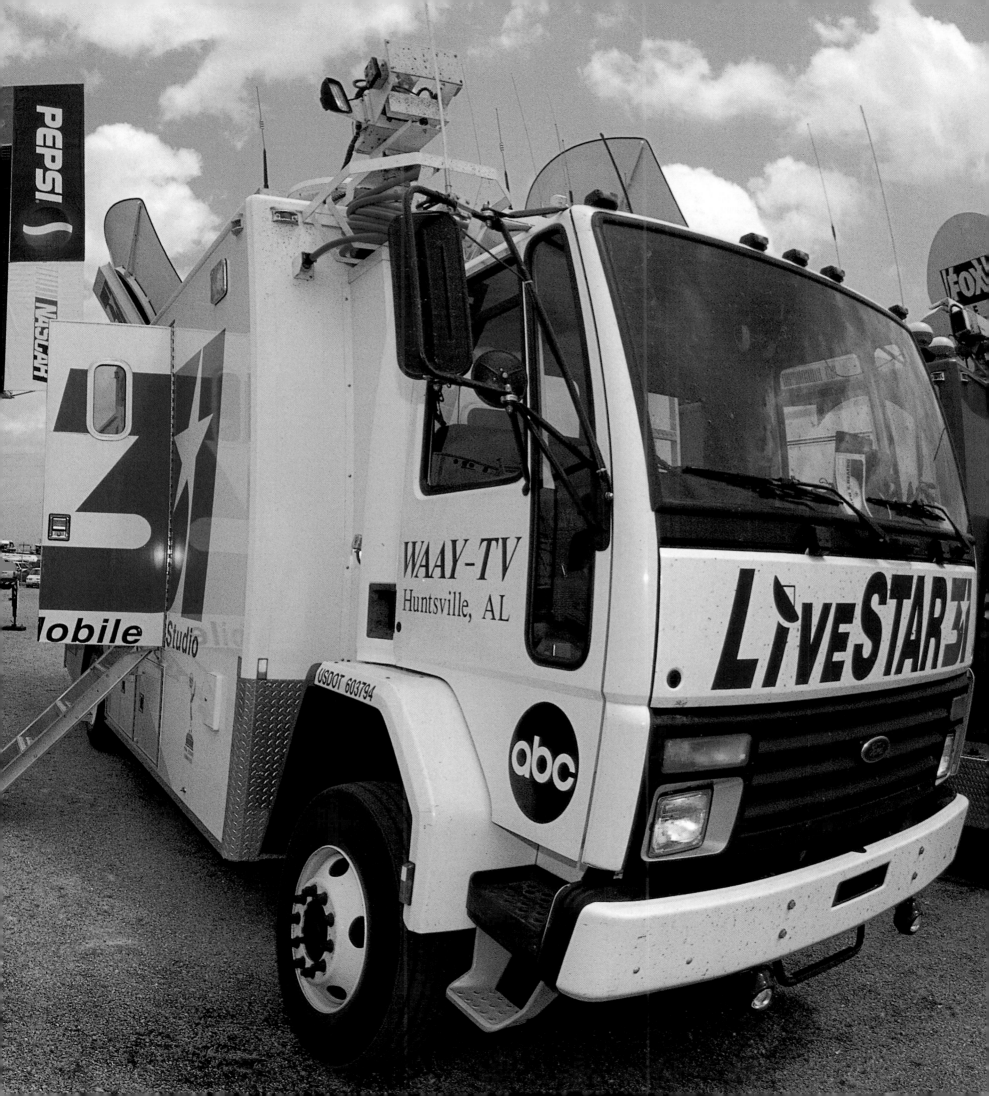

"The value that NASCAR and NBC Sports, TBS Superstation and Fox Sports and its subsidiary FX created is that events will now be presented to the fans in a very detailed, behind-the-scenes fashion, with more accessibility to the information that goes on," says NASCAR Senior Vice President and Chief Operating Officer Mike Helton. "They have a very large interest in doing more than just green flag to checkered flag. I think what NBC Sports and Fox Sports are committed to is delivering our product to the fans because they believe in it. Delivery of our product to the fans was critical to all of this. Accessibility and the quality of production was a very, very important part of this."

Maybe the biggest key to the deal is the money involved: Put simply, the way for NASCAR's television partners to recoup their multi-billion dollar investment is to increase the ratings of the races they broadcast. And there are but two ways to do that — increase promotion and improve quality.

(Left) When talking about communications, each of the teams has the capability to pick up satellite signals, allowing cable access and weather information at each and every track. Here, a satellite dish is being assembled for the No. 24 Hendrick Motorsports team. (Above) Television commentator Dick Berggren stands ready to relay information just before the start of the 2000 Daytona 500.

Despite rapidly advancing technology that brings fans ever closer to the action, NASCAR racing is still about good, close competition among the best drivers in the world.

When NBC Sports, Turner Sports, Fox Sports and FX take over in 2001, NASCAR will receive a tremendous amount of new network exposure. Turner alone has scheduled more than 4,000 commercial spots on TNT, TBS, CNN, Cartoon Network and other affiliated cable channels. NASCAR promos are also certain to air on popular NBC and Fox prime-time shows, including "Friends," "Ally McBeal" and "X Files."

A quick peek through the gate gets one young fan's mental wheels spinning almost as fast as those bolted to the race cars he is watching in the garage area.

(Left) Chad Little happily signs an autograph for one of his admirers. (Below left) Dr. Jerry Punch interviews Mark Martin before the start of a race. (Below Right) Fans settle in for another weekend of racing activity.

In short, fans will see NASCAR everywhere!

"You're going to be looking back at NASCAR in 10 years time and saying this is where the growth really started," says Fox Sports Television Group Chairman and Chief Executive Officer David Hill.

"This is a tremendous milestone, maybe the biggest since the founding of NASCAR more than 50 years ago," agrees Lowe's Motor Speedway President H.A. "Humpy" Wheeler. "Fox and NBC bring a new creativity to NASCAR racing. I think Fox and NBC will bring an intensity level to our coverage that will match such sports as the NFL and NBA. There is a tremendous amount of high drama in NASCAR racing which will be even more evident by this increase in network media intensity."

On the quality front, NASCAR and its television partners are taking a multifaceted approach, adding more pre- and post-race coverage for every event, as well as sharing any and all technological advancements among its television partners.

And those technological advancements will be stunning.

(Left) Although computers are not allowed in the cars during competition, electronic technology is very evident in the pits and in the garage as a means of providing teams with critical information. (Right) Photographers get a bird's-eye view from inside the orange 76 ball at Daytona International Speedway, just above a radio commentator perched close to the action on the track.

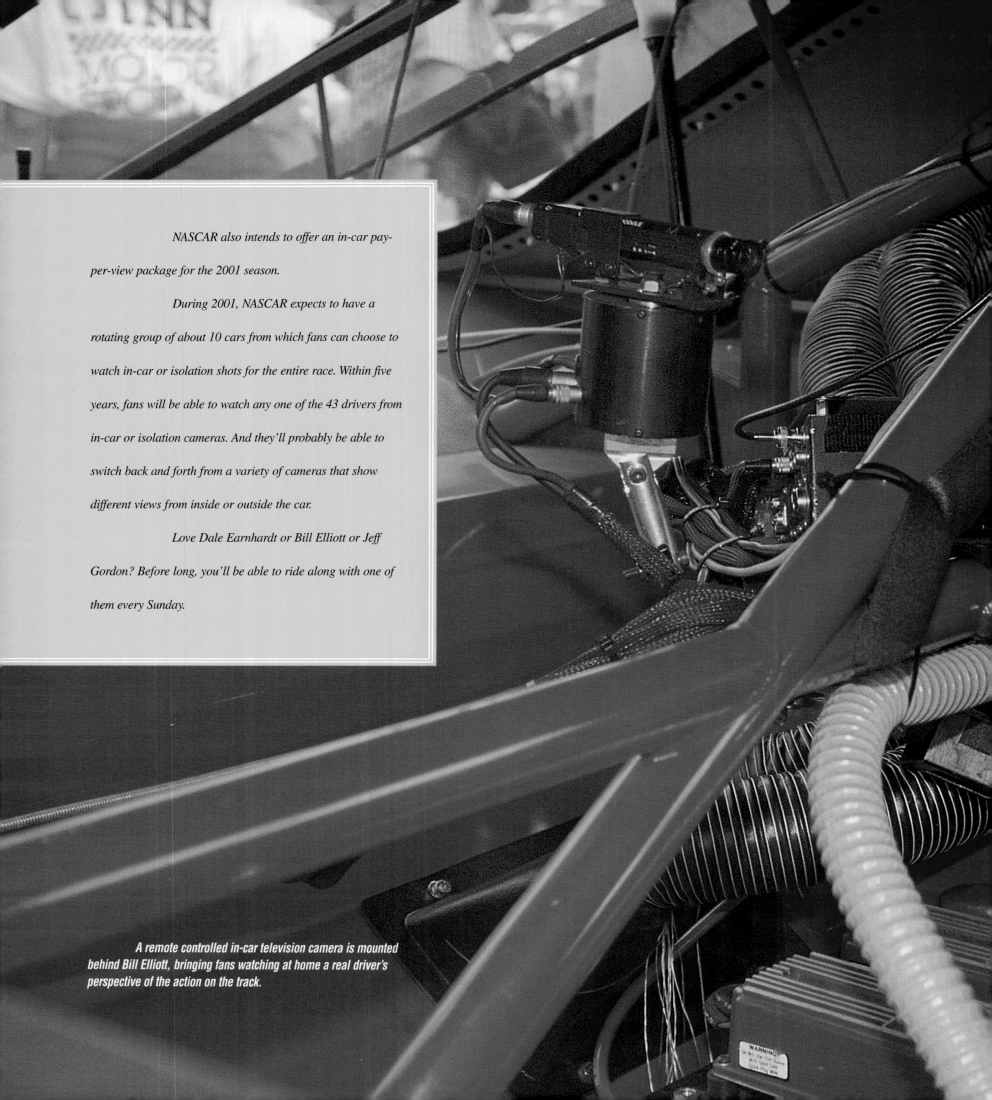

NASCAR also intends to offer an in-car pay-per-view package for the 2001 season.

During 2001, NASCAR expects to have a rotating group of about 10 cars from which fans can choose to watch in-car or isolation shots for the entire race. Within five years, fans will be able to watch any one of the 43 drivers from in-car or isolation cameras. And they'll probably be able to switch back and forth from a variety of cameras that show different views from inside or outside the car.

Love Dale Earnhardt or Bill Elliott or Jeff Gordon? Before long, you'll be able to ride along with one of them every Sunday.

A remote controlled in-car television camera is mounted behind Bill Elliott, bringing fans watching at home a real driver's perspective of the action on the track.

Eventually, electronic game manufacturers will be able to use advanced global positioning satellite technology to track exactly where every car is at every second on a race track and use that information to create more sophisticated driving games!

It's hard to believe how far and how fast TV already has come, and it's no exaggeration to say that the new TV deal is the biggest in NASCAR's history. The money is huge and so is the exposure for the sport and the new benefits and features for race fans.

Starting with Speedweeks in 2001, fans will never watch a NASCAR race the same way again.

"It was a nice day. It's been a long time coming," NASCAR President Bill France Jr. said when the new TV deal was announced in

late 1999. *"Our champions will be household words like Michael Jordan is, for instance. So that part of it's going to be real good. Even better than it's been."*

"This really does take us to where the NBA, the NFL and Major League Baseball are as far as the TV package and how the public perceives us," adds veteran racer Kyle Petty. *"I think that's incredible. This is huge for the sport."*

And what of the billions of dollars involved? "Fifty years from now these numbers we're trotting out will sound like a 35-cent loaf of bread that existed back in the 1930s," France laughed.

Huge crowds that pack the stands as well as the infields at NASCAR Winston Cup Series events are nothing new, but now, with the enhanced and expanded TV coverage set to begin in 2001, millions more will begin to enjoy the sport while watching at home.

The NASCAR Channel

One of the most exciting developments for race fans is the advent of The NASCAR Channel.

The NASCAR Channel will provide programming covering virtually all forms of NASCAR racing. It will be offered as a basic cable and satellite service.

During the week, there will be a one-hour nightly NASCAR news show, as well as a live personality-driven show featuring drivers, owners and crew members. In addition, The NASCAR Channel will highlight certain drivers during any given week, including features on that driver every night. One week might be devoted to news, history, and features about Dale Earnhardt, the next about Jeff Gordon.

In addition to expanded event coverage provided by NBC Sports, TBS Superstation and Fox Sports and their subsidiary FX, the NASCAR Channel will bring the fans closer than ever to the action that takes place during race weekends.

The NASCAR Channel also will carry reruns of all NASCAR Winston Cup Series, NASCAR Busch Series, Grand National Division and NASCAR Craftsman Truck Series races during the week, and provide fans with exposure to a host of races from NASCAR's numerous Touring Series and NASCAR Weekly Racing Series events from across the nation.

Perhaps the most exciting element is the depth of coverage The NASCAR Channel will be able to provide at NASCAR Winston Cup Series events.

On Sundays, fans will be able to sit at home and watch The NASCAR Channel on their televisions and look in on the drivers meeting, chapel service and tech inspections. Post-race tech inspection and live coverage from victory lane also will be included on The NASCAR Channel.

Lists are a big part of NASCAR racing, as they assure everything is done to the race car before the event is scheduled to begin. (Inset) Fuel mileage can be the difference between winning and losing a race. Here, Jerry Schweitz of Team Sabco jots down some vital numbers on team charts.

All told, The NASCAR Channel and NASCAR's new television partners will bring new and old fans alike a level of access and information about the sport that simply was never conceivable before, let alone available.

"As soon as people understand our sport, they're hooked as fans," says NASCAR Vice President of Broadcasting & Technology Bray Cary. "So what we want to do is use TV to simplify that process for the new person who may not want to invest as much time, and yet not take anything away from our core group of fans who really love and understand the sport."

(Left) Veteran MRN announcer Jim Phillips shares a laugh with seven-time NASCAR Winston Cup Series Champion Dale Earnhardt. (Below) Some very expensive machines are used to get each and every part of a NASCAR Winston Cup Series ride as close to perfect as humanly possible. Computer-driven machining equipment like this allows teams to precisely manufacture many of their own parts. (Bottom) Some adjustments only require an inexpensive tool or two to get the job done, but precision and thoroughness are always required.

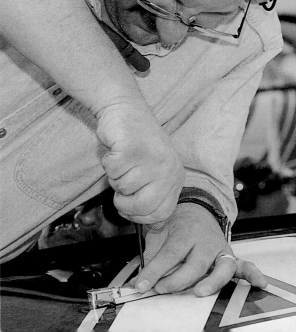

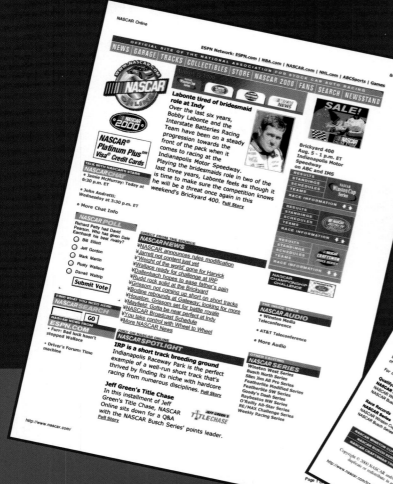

NASCAR Online

As dramatic as the television enhancements are, the potential of NASCAR Online is virtually limitless. Already, NASCAR Online is the sanctioning body's official Internet site and the most popular website in auto racing. Just by clicking onto NASCAR Online at http://www.nascar.com, readers can find a host of information: News, statistics, results and standings for NASCAR Winston Cup Series, NASCAR Busch Series and NASCAR Craftsman Truck Series races are readily available, as is secure shopping at the NASCAR Online Store.

In addition, there are regular driver chats, fan polls, audio and video clips, race photos and updates from other NASCAR series.

And that's just for starters.

One of the newest steps to get NASCAR to the public is via the Internet, where features, news, statistics and on-line shopping can be found. NASCAR.com will also offer real-time scoring, in-car telemetry and monitoring of team frequencies during events.

As television and Internet technologies begin to converge, online options will increase dramatically.

Online chats will be like video conferences — you'll actually see and talk to drivers live through your computer.

NASCAR Online users will be able to order video on demand, which will allow them to view old races whenever they want to. There will be links on NASCAR Online to driver sites, track sites, fantasy games, fan clubs and games.

Of course, during races NASCAR Online will have real-time scoring and telemetry to allow fans to keep up with the races even if they can't get to a television.

NASCAR Online also will be the definitive source for driver and team merchandise. "It will be the only place in the world that you can get anything from any driver," Cary promises. "That's what our goal is. No other place."

Central to the development of NASCAR Online will be high-speed Internet access, which should be in about 70 percent of homes across America within three years.

Fans attending races can look for benefits, too. As so-called "wireless" Internet service improves and becomes more commonplace in the near future, laptop computers and cellular telephones with Internet capability eventually will help fans follow their favorite drivers and teams that much closer.

The XM NASCAR Channel

      In January 2000, NASCAR and XM Satellite Radio announced plans to create the nation's first 24-hour, seven-day-a-week, all-NASCAR radio channel exclusively for XM Radio. The deal also included a strategic marketing relationship giving XM Radio an extensive sales/merchandising presence at each NASCAR event.

      The XM NASCAR channel will focus on the total NASCAR lifestyle and experience: the races, cars, drivers, fans, collectibles, behind-the-scenes interviews and features, and in-depth analysis of all NASCAR events.

      XM Satellite Radio is developing a new band of radio, targeted to launch in 2001. XM Radio will create up to 100 channels of digital-quality music, news, sports, talk and children's programming, which will be uplinked to XM Radio's satellites and transmitted directly to vehicle, home and portable radios coast-to-coast for a monthly subscription fee of $9.95.

(Right) At some of the smaller tracks, crews use pit road to make adjustments on their cars during practice sessions, giving fans a clear view of activities often confined to the garage area. Here, the NASCAR Busch Series teams of Dave Blaney (no. 93) and Mike McLaughlin (No. 34) make chassis changes and replace tires during practice at South Boston in 1999.

(Above) Souvenirs of all types can be purchased right at trackside. (Below) Announcing one's loyalty to a specific team or driver can be displaced in a variety of ways — some quite creative.

Sponsors and Fans

Obviously, this new broadcast and computer technology opens up a whole new series of ways for sponsors and race fans to interact.

More fertile ground — pun intended — for virtual reality ads can be found on the infield of some larger tracks. Indianapolis Motor Speedway already has had ads projected onto the grassy area between its turns during at least one running of the Brickyard 400.

With the new NASCAR Channel on television and the XM NASCAR Channel on radio, there will be many opportunities for new sponsors to come into the sport, or existing ones to branch out into new ways of reaching fans.

And as the technology to reach fans becomes more sophisticated, so will the techniques advertisers use to communicate information and measure end results.

The Bottom Line

The pace of technological change in the world is stupefying, and so is the change race fans will see in years ahead. And although some of the advances may seem like they are straight out of a sci-fi fantasy world, they are very real indeed. And they will give race fans a degree of access to and knowledge about the sport that can only serve to enhance the experience all that much more, bringing them closer than ever to NASCAR racing.

When at the track, hundreds of thousands of race fans gather each weekend to enjoy their sport. NASCAR is truly the fastest growing spectator sport in America.

NASCAR

(LEFT) 1999 NASCAR WINSTON CUP SERIES CHAMPION DALE JARRETT PROUDLY DISPLAYS HIS TROPHY PRIOR TO THE NASCAR AWARDS

WINSTON CUP

BANQUET AND CEREMONY IN NEW YORK CITY. (ABOVE) RED BYRON STANDS WITH HIS "STRICTLY STOCK" MACHINE IN 1949,

SERIES CHAMPS

THE YEAR HE BECAME NASCAR'S FIRST CHAMPION IN WHAT IS NOW THE NASCAR WINSTON CUP SERIES.

The Waldorf-Astoria
22
Miller
HIGH
LIFE
GOODYEAR
Edelbrock
Winston
DieHard
CHAMPION
REED
MONROE
MOOG
MOROSO
STP
EARL'S
Goody's
UNION
EAGLE

BOBBY *ALLISON*

When Bobby Allison won the 1983 NASCAR Winston Cup Series championship, it was the crowning point of a career that had spanned 18 seasons competing on the full schedule.

After five runner-up finishes in the championship chase, and in only his second year with DiGard Racing Co., crew chief Gary Nelson and engine builder Robert Yates, Allison's 1983 season was highlighted by six victories and 25 finishes among the top 10. Allison's climb to the championship was powered by a hot September, in which he won three races in a row — at Darlington, Richmond and Dover. Adding luster to his year was the fact he was named the NASCAR Winston Cup Series Most Popular Driver for the fourth consecutive year.

Allison was honored at the NASCAR Awards Banquet in New York, where he received a phone call from President Ronald Reagan and a visit from Vice President George Bush.

An accident at Pocono Raceway in 1988 cut Allison's career short but by then, he had already won 84 races to put him in a tie for third place on NASCAR's all-time winners' list.

BUCK
BAKER

Buck Baker received a phone call from legendary team owner Carl Kiekhaefer in January of 1956 inquiring if Baker would like to become the driver for one of Kiekhaefer's Chryslers. Baker accepted, and his career boomed.

As a member of the Kiekhaefer juggernaut in 1956, Baker won 14 of 48 starts and wound up among the top 10 a whopping 39 times to earn the first NASCAR Winston Cup Series title of his career. But he wasn't done yet.

Despite his championship, Baker left the Kiekhaefer organiza-tion to run his own Chevrolets in 1957. He had a remarkable season. He won 10 times in 40 starts and finished in the top 10 a remarkable 38 times en route to his second straight NASCAR Winston Cup Series title. At one stretch during the latter half of 1956 and the first eight months of 1957, Baker finished among the top 10 in 35 consecutive events, a NASCAR record.

His last full season as a driver was in 1968. However, the sturdy Charlotte, N.C., native continued to run in selected races until 1976.

RED BYRON

In 1949, NASCAR ran its first official NASCAR Winston Cup Series season, called "Strictly Stock" back then. It consisted of just eight races, beginning with a 200-lapper at Charlotte Speedway on June 19.

By the time NASCAR began, Robert "Red" Byron had already established a reputation as a rugged, no-holds-barred driver. In NASCAR, he displayed his talent quickly. He was the circuit's National Modified champion in 1948. On the fledgling "Strictly Stock" tour a year later, he won the second race

of the year on the Daytona Beach sand and road course. He entered only five more races in that inaugural season and compiled a record of two wins and four finishes among the top 10.

That was more than enough to make him the very first NASCAR Winston Cup Series champion, which has established him as a significant part of NASCAR lore, even though he ran in just nine more races through 1951 before departing NASCAR.

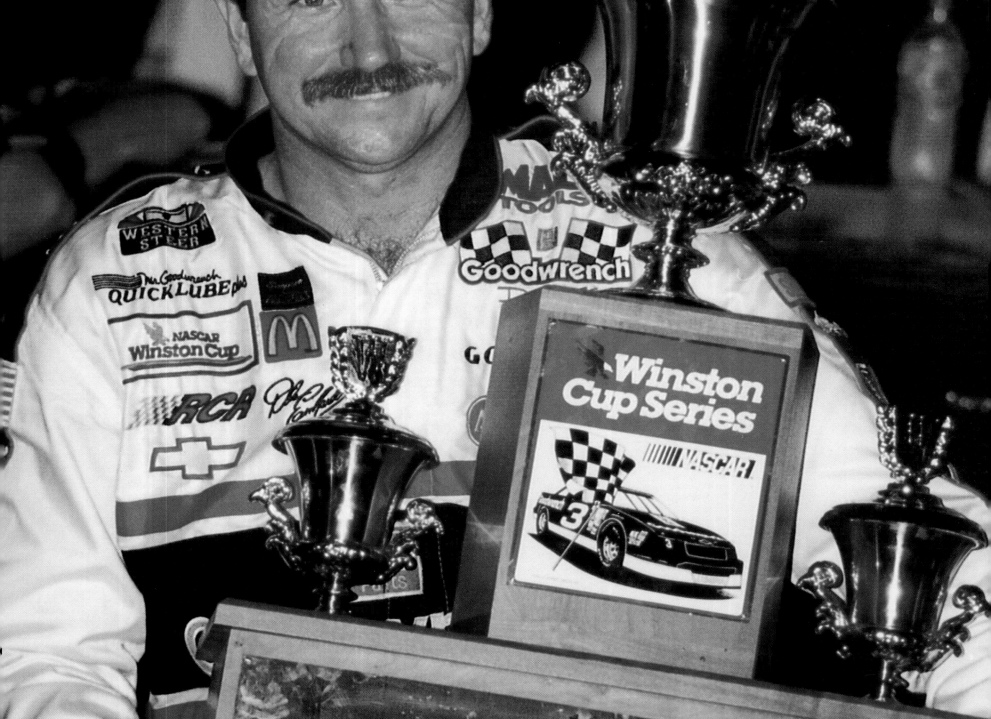

1993
Winston Cup Champion
Dale Earnhardt

DALE EARNHARDT

1980
1986
1987
1990
1991
1993
1994

Dale Earnhardt learned his lessons well from his father, NASCAR Sportsman Champion Ralph Earnhardt — considered one of the toughest competitors in the sport's history.

Embarking on his own career, young Earnhardt found it difficult. It wasn't until he caught a break in 1979 that he ascended to the heights. That year, he was given the wheel of Rod Osterlund's Chevrolets and proceeded to win his first NASCAR Winston Cup Series race at Bristol, Tenn. He then roared ahead to capture the NASCAR Winston Cup Series Rookie of the Year title.

One year later and still with Osterlund, he won his first career NASCAR Winston Cup Series title. He remains the only driver to win the rookie of the year and a championship in consecutive seasons.

After a three-year lull, Earnhardt joined Richard Childress Racing in 1984 and the rest, as they say, is history. From then until the present, Earnhardt sped to six more titles - 1986, '87, '90, '91, '93, '94 — to tie Richard Petty for the most career NASCAR Winston Cup Series championships.

1983
Winston Cup Champi

BILL ELLIOTT

No driver in NASCAR Winston Cup Series history has been more popular than Bill Elliott, a lanky redhead from Dawsonville, Ga. Elliott's legion of fans have voted him the NASCAR Winston Cup Series Most Popular Driver 14 times in the last 16 years, prior to the conclusion of the 2000 campaign. A big reason why is Elliott's impressive record as a driver.

In 1985, in his fourth season with team owner Harry Melling, Elliott astounded the racing world by winning 11 pole positions and 11 super-speedway races. After winning the Southern 500 at Darlington Raceway that year,

Elliott claimed the first Winston Million bonus of $1 million. He had won three of the program's four selected races — at Daytona, Talladega and Darlington.

As spectacular as that was, Elliott built his NASCAR Winston Cup Series championship season of 1988 on the foundation of six victories and 22 finishes among the top 10. He became the first Ford driver to win the title since David Pearson in 1969.

After his championship effort, he was voted American Driver of the Year and Georgia Professional Athlete of the Year

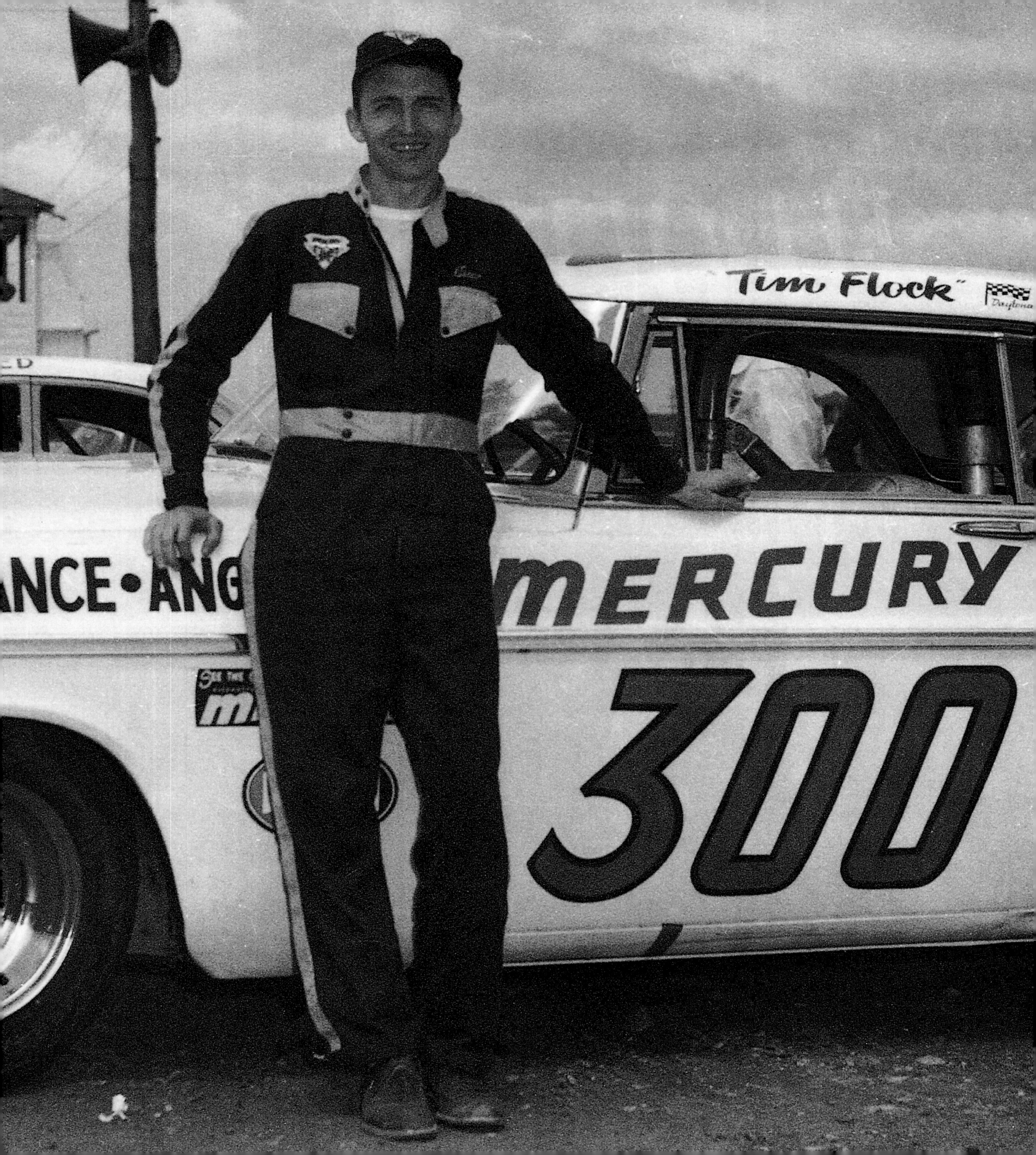
"Tim Flock"
Daytona
ANCE•ANG
MERCURY
300

TIM FLOCK

Fun-loving Tim Flock, one of NASCAR's great characters, drove a Hudson for team owner Ted Chester in 1952 and found himself locked in a ferocious duel for the NASCAR Winston Cup Series championship with Herb Thomas.

The two were separated by less than 200 points going into the season's last race at West Palm Beach on Nov. 30. In that race, on the 164th lap, Flock's Hudson hit the retaining wall and flipped over, skidding down the frontstretch on its roof. But it didn't matter. The title was Flock's. "I bet I'm the only guy who ever won a championship while on his head," Flock said. He won eight races and scored 25 top-10 finishes in 33 races in 1952.

Three years later, Flock was part of the powerful Carl Kiekhaefer organization and the association paid off handsomely. In a Kiekhaefer Chrysler, Flock won a remarkable 18 races and compiled 33 top-10 finishes in just 38 starts en route to his second career championship. In 1955, he was far and away the dominant driver on the Series. That year, no other driver won more than six races.

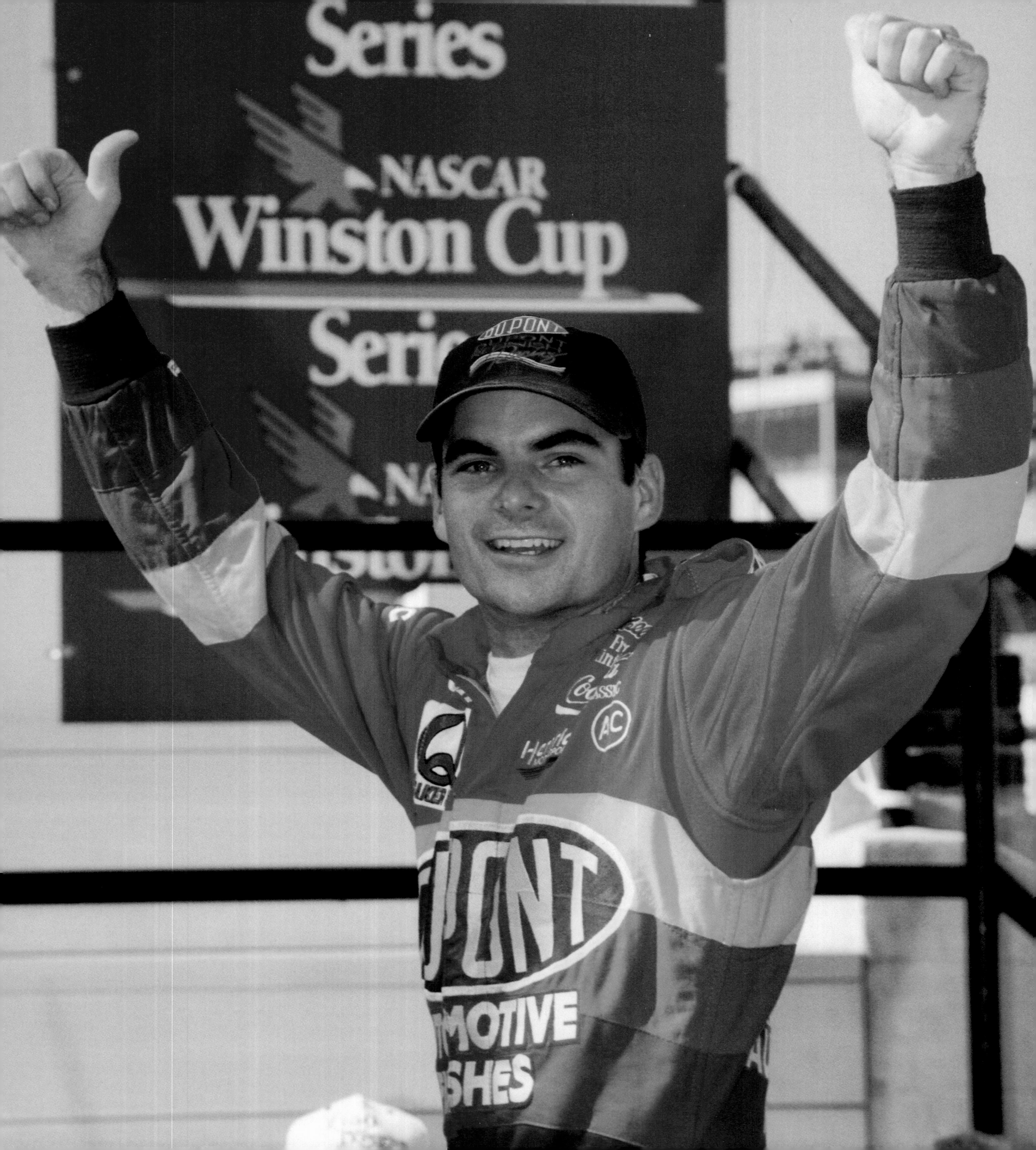
Series
NASCAR
Winston Cup
Series
DUPONT
AC
MOTIVE
SHES

JEFF GORDON

When Jeff Gordon, at just 21 years old, joined team owner Rick Hendrick in 1993, no one was prepared for what would transpire. They got a hint as he became the youngest driver ever to win a 125-Mile Qualifying Race for the Daytona 500 and breezed to the NASCAR Winston Cup Series Rookie of the Year title.

Two years later, he won seven races and had 23 finishes among the top 10. At 24, he became the second-youngest driver ever to win the coveted NASCAR Winston Cup Series championship.

He won 10 races in 1996 and finished second in the final point standings and a year later, he again won 10 races and this time was crowned champion for the second time in his career.

It was even better in 1998. That year, he won 13 races, tying Richard Petty for the modern-era record for most wins in a season. He also won the Winston No Bull 5 twice — earning $1 million each time — at Indianapolis and Darlington, and picked up his third career NASCAR Winston Cup Series crown.

BOBBY
ISAAC

A quiet, shy driver from Catawba, N.C., Bobby Isaac had won the North Carolina Sportsman championship and several track titles before he moved into the NASCAR Winston Cup Series in 1961.

By 1969, he was an established star with 17 victories that year. The following season, driving Nord Krauskopf-owned Dodges maintained by legendary crew chief Harry Hyde, Isaac won the NASCAR Winston Cup Series championship in dramatic fashion.

It wasn't until the next-to-last race of the season, at North Carolina Speedway in Rockingham, N.C., that Isaac clinched the title. He didn't have a spectacular finish by any means — he cruised home in seventh place — but it was enough to give him the championship by just 51 points over Bobby Allison. Isaac won 11 races and compiled 38 top-10 finishes in 47 starts that year.

In his championship season, Isaac established himself as the world's fastest stock car driver up to that time. He broke the world closed-course speed record at Talladega Superspeedway with a run of 201.104 mph in a Krauskopf Dodge in November.

DALE JARRETT

After several years of struggle on the NASCAR Winston Cup Series, Dale Jarrett got his big break in 1990, when he became the driver for the vaunted Wood Brothers team. A year later, at Michigan, he won his first career race.

In 1992, he pursued another opportunity and became the driver for the new Joe Gibbs Racing team. That led to a victory in the Daytona 500 in 1993.

Jarrett moved to Robert Yates Racing in 1995, and the association has been fruitful, to say the least. In 1997, Jarrett won seven races. In 1998,

he won a $1 million bonus in the Winston No Bull 5 with a victory at Talladega Superspeedway, and finished third in the final point standings.

Then, in 1999, Jarrett reached the pinnacle. He won the NASCAR Winston Cup Series championship on the heels of four victories and 29 finishes among the top 10. He failed to finish only one race in his title season.

He joined his father Ned as only the second father-son duo to win the NASCAR Winston Cup Series championship. Lee and Richard Petty were the first.

NED JARRETT

By 1961, Ned Jarrett, dubbed "Gentleman Ned" by his peers, had made just 57 starts on the NASCAR Winston Cup Series circuit, but had earned five victories and finished fifth in the final point standings.

He took the wheel of a Chevrolet in 1961 and set out to claim his first NASCAR Winston Cup Series championship. He earned the crown after the year's final race at Hillsboro, N.C. Jarrett won only one race in 1961, but parlayed consistency in the form of 34 top-10 finishes in 46 starts to earn the title.

From there, Jarrett's career continued to blossom, winning races in every year, including 15 in 1964. The following year, he won his second NASCAR Winston Cup Series title driving for team owner Bondy Long. He competed in 54 races and earned 13 victories, finishing among the top 10 a remarkable 45 times.

Jarrett raced just one more year, with only 21 starts, before retiring in his prime. His career record shows 50 wins, which ties him for eighth place on NASCAR Winston Cup Series' all-time list.

ALAN
KULWICKI

Alan Kulwicki was an anomaly in NASCAR Winston Cup Series racing, always choosing to own the cars he raced throughout his career. On a shoestring budget, the determined driver from Greenfield, Wis., won the Series' Rookie of the Year title in 1986.

He won his first race at Phoenix in 1988, and four years later, he found himself locked in the battle for the championship, which turned out to be the most dramatic in NASCAR history.

In the season's final race at Atlanta, Kulwicki went head-to-

head with Bill Elliott after title contender Davey Allison was eliminated in an accident on lap 254. Kulwicki knew his only chance to win the title was to lead the most laps and earn a five-point bonus. He led three times for 103 laps while Elliott led seven times for 102 laps and won the race.

But Kulwicki won the championship by a mere 10 points, the closest margin in NASCAR history.

Tragically, he lost his life in a plane crash near Blountville, Tenn., on April 1, 1993.

TERRY *LABONTE*

Team owner Billy Hagan gave Terry Labonte his big break in 1978, putting him in a NASCAR Winston Cup Series car. He won his first career race in 1980, and by 1984, had developed into a championship contender largely because of his consistent driving style that earned him the nickname, "The Iceman."

In 1984, he found himself locked in a battle for the championship with Harry Gant, that wasn't decided until the final race of the year, at Riverside, Calif. There, Labonte finished third and Gant eighth. The title was Labonte's by just 65 points. Labonte won only twice that year, but "The Iceman" finished among the top 10 a solid 24 times in 30 races.

Fast-forward to 1994. Labonte is now a member of Rick Hendrick's organization. Two years later, he won the championship for a second time — and in much the same fashion as he won his first. He won only two races, but had 24 top-10 finishes in 31 races, including 21 in the top five.

Labonte's championships came 12 years apart. That's the most years between championships in NASCAR history.

BENNY
PARSONS

Benny Parsons goes down in history as the driver to win a NASCAR Winston Cup Series championship in the most dramatic fashion.

It happened in the 28th race of the 1973 season, the American 500 at Rockingham, N.C. Parsons entered the race with a 194.35-point lead over Richard Petty in the standings.

However, on the 13th lap of the race, Parsons' L.G. DeWitt-owned Chevrolet was torn up in an accident. The entire right side of the car was ripped away. Parsons' day seemed over and the championship lost.

But Parsons' team and members of several other teams rallied around him. Working feverishly in the garage area and using parts taken from cars that had not made the field, they patched Parson's car back together and he re-entered the race 136 laps after the accident happened.

He limped home in 28th place, good enough to give him the championship by 67.15 points.

"What those guys did for me," Parsons said at the time, "was a miracle." And that's the way racing history records it.

DAVID *PEARSON*

By 1966, David Pearson had won 13 NASCAR Winston Cup Series races and the 1960 Rookie of the Year title. In 1966, Pearson blistered the Series, winning 15 times in 42 starts to cruise to the championship by nearly 2,000 points over James Hylton.

Pearson drove for the Holman-Moody team in 1968, and again ripped the competition. En route to his second career title, he won 16 times and scored 38 finishes among the top 10 in 47 races.

It was pretty much the same thing in 1969, when Pearson won his third title with 11 victories and a whopping 44 top-10 finishes in 51 races.

Although he didn't win another title, Pearson went on to great things, particularly during his years with the Wood Brothers, with whom he ran a limited schedule. In 1973, he stunned the NASCAR world with 11 superspeedway wins in just 18 starts.

In his career, Pearson won 105 races, second only to Richard Petty in NASCAR history.

LEE PETTY

When Lee Petty began racing out of his shops in Level Cross, N.C., in 1949, he probably had no idea he would be the father of a dynasty.

By 1954, Lee had already won 11 NASCAR Winston Cup Series races. The 1954 campaign would be his best. He won seven times and piled up an incredible 32 finishes among the top 10 in 34 races, winning the championship by nearly 300 points over Herb Thomas.

Four years later, and just about the time son Richard was going to get behind the wheel, the elder Petty campaigned an Oldsmobile. In 50 races,

he won seven times and finished 44 times among the top 10 — again an incredible record of consistency — to earn his second NASCAR Winston Cup Series championship.

In 1959, Petty became a part of NASCAR history as he won the inaugural Daytona 500, nipping Johnny Beauchamp in a photo finish. That year, Petty won 11 times in 42 races, with 35 top-10 finishes. That was more than enough to give him his third NASCAR Winston Cup Series crown.

RICHARD *PETTY*

1964
1967
1971
1972
1974
1975
1979

Richard Petty first got behind the wheel of a race car in 1958, and by the time he won his first Series championship, he had already won 27 races. In 1964, he entered 61 events and won nine of them with 43 top-10 finishes to run away with his first title.

His second championship came in 1967, a year that defies description. In 48 starts, Petty won an astonishing 27 times, including a string of 10 races in a row, and was dubbed "The King," a title that remained with him throughout his career.

It was much the same in 1971, with 21 wins in 46 starts. He won consecutive titles in 1974 and 1975, and his seventh and final championship came in 1979. It was, for a change, a squeaker, with Petty beating Darrell Waltrip by only 11 points, the second-closest margin in NASCAR history.

Petty continued to race through 1992. When his career came to an end, he had won 200 races, more than any other driver in NASCAR history.

BILL REXFORD

Only 19 point races were held in 1950, and while some legendary drivers made headlines with multiple victories, it was a very young man out of upstate New York who claimed the championship and became the second titlist in NASCAR history.

Bill Rexford was an unlikely candidate for the crown, given the roster of veterans who raced against him. But he took on the challenge and ran in 17 races in an Oldsmobile. His lone victory came at Canfield, Ohio, on a half-mile dirt track. However, he coupled that win with 11 finishes among the top 10.

In the season's final race at Hillsboro, N.C., Rexford and Fireball Roberts were in contention for the title. Rexford seemed to put it in Roberts' hands when his engine blew and he finished 26th. All Roberts had to do was finish fifth and the championship was his.

But Roberts threw caution to the wind and his engine failed after 126 laps. Under the system of the day, neither Rexford nor Roberts received points for their finishes and thus, Rexford, who had just turned 24, became the youngest NASCAR Winston Cup Series champion in history.

HERB *THOMAS*

Herb Thomas is part of NASCAR lore as a member of that early contingent of drivers — including Buck Baker, Curtis Turner, Marshall Teague and others — who served as racing pioneers.

Thomas became only the third NASCAR Winston Cup Series champion in 1951, driving one of the thundering Hudson Hornets of the day. He competed in 34 of the season's 41 races and won seven times, including the second Southern 500 at Darlington Raceway. He earned the championship by just over 146 points ahead of chief rival Fonty Flock.

Thomas continued to campaign Hudsons over the next two years and in 1953, he established a record by winning 12 races over the course of the season. He also earned 31 finishes among the top 10 in a year when Hudsons won 22 of 37 races. With his second career championship, the native of Olivia, N.C., earned nearly $29,000 in purse and point money, the most in NASCAR's short history.

Thomas continued to race until 1962. He earned 48 career victories, which puts him 10th on the all-time list.

DARRELL *WALTRIP*

1981
1982
1985

Darrell Waltrip got the break he needed in 1975 when he joined DiGard Racing where, from 1975-1980, he won 26 times.

But it was in 1981 he got the opportunity of his career. Team owner Junior Johnson hired Waltrip. And history was made.

Their first year together produced 12 victories and Waltrip's first championship. It would prove to be no fluke. In 1982, Johnson and Waltrip did it again — another 12 victories and a second-straight title.

Waltrip continued to win and in 1985, he overcame a large point deficit to win his third career title. With only 10 races remaining in the season, Waltrip trailed point-leader Bill Elliott by 143 points. But he came charging forward. In the last race of the season at Riverside, Calif., Waltrip finished seventh while mechanical problems dropped Elliott to 31st. Waltrip won the title by 101 points.

Since then, Waltrip has gone on to carve his place in NASCAR history with 84 career victories, which ties him for third on the all-time list.

RUSTY WALLACE

Rusty Wallace brought his aggressive racing style, honed on short tracks in the Midwest, to NASCAR Winston Cup Series racing full-time in 1984. Driving for team owner Cliff Stewart, he won the Rookie of the Year title.

It was two years later, when Wallace became the driver for Raymond Beadle's team, that his career ascended. He won twice in his first year with Beadle, two more times in 1987 and six times in 1988. He was poised for a NASCAR Winston Cup Series championship.

In 1989, he again won six races. But he also had 20 finishes among the top 10 in 29 races. For most of the season, he dueled with friend Dale Earnhardt for the championship and it wasn't decided until the final race of the year at Atlanta. Wallace entered the race as the point leader and needed to finish within 19 positions of Earnhardt to claim the title.

Earnhardt romped to victory and Wallace had one problem after another. But he survived them nicely and finished 15th, thereby earning the 1989 NASCAR Winston Cup Series championship.

JOE WEATHERLY

He was the "Clown Prince of Racing," a man who liked to drive cars fast and lead the fast life.

Virginia-born Joe Weatherly had been racing in NASCAR for just about as long as there was a NASCAR, first trying his luck in 1952. But he didn't get into it full-time until 1962, when he entered 52 races as the driver of Bud Moore's Pontiac based in Spartanburg, S.C.

Weatherly got the chance to shine. He won nine races and finished 45 times among the top 10. That garnered him his first NASCAR Winston Cup Series championship.

It didn't end there. Weatherly again teamed up with Moore in 1963. This time, he ran in 53 races yet won only three times. However, his 35 top-10 finishes were the deciding factor as he claimed a second-straight crown.

Weatherly's last victory came on Oct. 27, 1963 at Hillsboro, N.C. He and Moore were poised to make another run at the championship in 1964, but it all came to end in the year's fifth race at Riverside, Calif., where Weatherly lost his life in an accident.

REX
WHITE

In 1960, as drivers such as Curtis Turner, Junior Johnson, Fireball Roberts and a young Richard Petty were holding sway, it might be correct to say no one paid Rex White a lot of attention. They should have.

White, then 31 years old, had made limited starts in NASCAR beginning in 1956. He had won seven races from 1956-1959 and decided to embark on the full schedule in 1960.

He made 40 starts that year and piled up six victories, all on short tracks. His consistency was remarkable. He finished in the top 10 a healthy 35 times. He rolled over the bigger names as he sped to the championship, winning it by a whopping 3,936 points over Petty.

White bid for a second title in 1961, and won even more races — seven in 47 starts. But it wasn't good enough and he finished second in the final point standings, behind champion Ned Jarrett.

In 1962, White won eight times in 37 races, his best record, but could do no better than fifth in points. He closed his career after the 1964 season.

CALE YARBOROUGH

1976
1977
1978

When Bobby Allison departed Junior Johnson after a successful 1972 campaign, Johnson was looking for the kind of driver he liked — aggressive. He found him in Cale Yarborough.

Together, they formed the most dominant team of the decade.

Yarborough won four races in 1973, his first with Johnson. He won 10 in 1974 and three more in 1975. Then, in 1976, Yarborough sped to nine victories and won his first NASCAR Winston Cup Series championship. In 1977, he won nine more races and claimed a second consecutive title.

After driving Johnson's Chevrolet over several years, Yarborough switched to an Oldsmobile in 1978. The result? Another 10 victories and a third-straight championship, this one by nearly 500 points over Allison.

Yarborough remained with Johnson through 1980 and together they won 49 races along with those three titles — one of the most successful driver-owner combinations in NASCAR history.

He ended his career after the 1988 season with 83 wins, fifth on NASCAR's all-time list.

NASCAR FANS'

(LEFT) EIGHT-YEAR-OLD MICHAEL CHEMRIS OF HOWELL, N.J., IS READY FOR THE ACTION TO BEGIN AT MARTINSVILLE, DOCUMENTED IN THIS PHOTO

CANDID VIEW OF

TAKEN BY MICHAEL'S DAD THOMAS CHEMRIS. (ABOVE) BANNERS WAVE HIGH ABOVE THE INFIELD CROWD AT DAYTONA. PHOTO BY DAVID CHOBAT.

THEIR SPORT

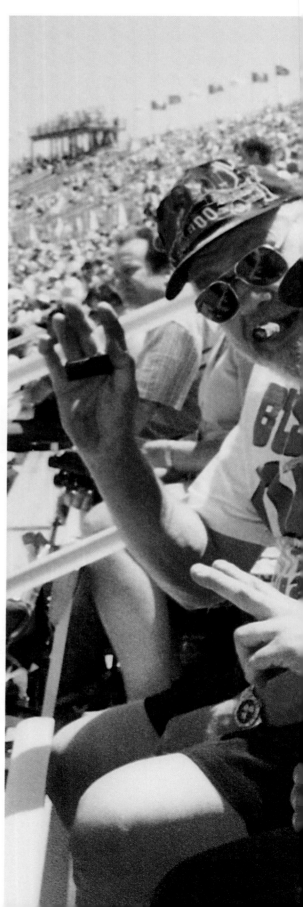

(Left) Salem, New Hampshire's Doug Garron set the timer on his camera to snap this shot of himself hanging around with a few of his "buddies." (Left, Below) A little rain doesn't bother Carrie and Joshua Vlietstra after they made the trek to Michigan Speedway from their home in Kalamazoo to see their first NASCAR Winston Cup Series event. Carrie and Joshua's mother – and veteran race fan – Deb Vlietstra captured this family moment on film. (Below) Mary Meikel caught her gang's attention and clicked this one before a race at California Speedway. Pictured are (from left) friends Paul Obermeyer and Jay Obermeyer, who joined Mary on the trip from their homes in Connersville, Ind., and Mary's son Troy Meikel with grandkids Rex and Lindsay Meikel of nearby Riverside, Calif.

(Above) Joseph Motil of Tampa, Fla., checks out practice for the Pocono 500 from atop the Team Sabco transporter. Joining Joseph for the occasion was his mother, Marie Motil from Harwood, Pa., who did a nice job of adding a patriotic theme to her photo. (Right) There's no doubt who five-and-a-half-year-old Elly Korbelik pulls for. Elly's mom Ronda Korbelik of Ronda's Photography in Milligan, Neb., put this nice shot together.

Adam Feinberg and Allison Sher of Philadelphia, Pa., were photographed at Daytona by friend George King. Allison is holding a copy of NASCAR Winston Cup Scene, in which Adam had placed a classified ad containing his marriage proposal to her. When she finished reading the ad, Adam presented her an engagement ring, which quickly went on her finger. The happy couple plans to wed in April 2001.

(Left) Lois Schmidt of Kettering, Ohio, sent us this picture of husband Steve Schmidt enjoying a morning tailgate breakfast during their annual trip to Bristol, Tenn. (Below) Photographer David Chobat thought this group of enthusiastic fans had a very nice "corner lot" outside Martinsville Speedway in southern Virginia. (Bottom) These self-proclaimed "NASCAR Fanatics" were photographed by Jessica Ward of Wichita, Kan. Pictured are (from left) Terry Powers, Carl Leonard, Lisa Powers, Mark Powers, Diane Leonard, Mark McBeth, Vicki Trimm and Steve Trimm (in red hat). Carl Leonard painted the trailer, which the gang pulls to the races behind their motor home.

(Left) There's never a lack of enthusiasm in the grandstands at a NASCAR Winston Cup Series event. These fans decided to warm up for the race by practicing The Wave, captured on film by photographer Don Grassman. (Top) Veteran race-goer Roger Heidenescher of Columbus, Ohio, photographed (from left) friends Joann and Warren Crites with Roger's wife Cathy – the "September Birthday Trio" – during their visit to Bristol. This gang says, "Real fans CROSS the finish line to meet their drivers." (Above) Maryland's Joseph Butler caught his brother, Webster "A. Buck" Butler of Niceville, Fla., quietly anticipating the day's activities hours before an event at Dover.

(Left) Joyce Smith of Bluemont, Va., focused on husband, William "Smitty" Smith, intently watching the action at Martinsville. Notice the reflection in Smitty's glasses – nice job Joyce! (Right) Seven-year-old Michelle Daugherty didn't miss the opportunity to show her support for No. 3, Dale Earnhardt, while attending The Winston. Michelle is being hoisted by her dad Kevin, while sister Katie (wearing red in front) cheers for her favorite driver, Dale Earnhardt Jr. Michelle's mom Tina Daugherty from Dickson, Tenn., took the photo.

You can see some pretty wild vehicles at NASCAR events, but this one may have 'em all beat. Brian Davis of Sarasota, Fla., spent 420 hours building this beauty, which he calls a cross between a reptile and a devil. Photo by David Chobat.

(Above) While visiting Las Vegas in March 2000, photographer Thom Higgins of Brentwood, Calif., caught Jim Burnett trying to "lift" the largest NASCAR Winston Cup Series trophy he's ever seen. (Left) This group of fans turned the tables on our photographer David Chobat outside victory lane after the Coca-Cola 600 at Lowe's Motor Speedway. (Below) Marsha Powers of Wichita, Kan., sent us this shot of Brittney (left) and P.J., who weren't about to be left at home when the family headed to Texas. When they're not at the races, the two dogs enjoy knee-boarding behind the family SeaDoo.

(Above) Tina Daugherty of Dickson, Tenn., snapped this shot of husband Kevin standing beside his favorite driver's car, specially-painted the 2000 edition of The Winston. (Right) Stephanie McCormick captured three of her colorful friends during their trip to Talladega from their homes in McMinnville, Tenn. Pictured are (from left) Brad Allison, Rodney Robinson and Todd Bless. (Below) Car owner Donnie Lerch of Cedar Rapids, Iowa, is well prepared if his favorite driver, Dale Earnhardt, decides to try his hand at mini stocks. Shelly Wilson, also of Cedar Rapids, submitted this photo, but says she has always preferred to root for Darrell Waltrip.

(Left) Lynne Gregory of Waynesboro, Va., found team owner Robert Yates in the garage area at Pocono and had her husband, Matthew, snap this shot for the family album. Lynne is no rookie when it comes to racing; she was a first-prize finalist for 1997 Sears DieHard/MRN NASCAR Fan of the Year. (Below) Deborah King gets a chance to meet Jeff Gordon after she was the first to register at a bone marrow drive held at Gordon's Chevrolet dealership in her town of Wilmington, N.C.

(Right) Terry Blehm of Lodi, Calif., took this photo of his wife, Michele, who is all smiles about having the opportunity to pose with her favorite driver, Michael Waltrip, at California Speedway. (Below) A chilly Texas breeze does not deter Diane Leonard (left) and Marsha Powers from checking in on pre-race activities prior to the 2000 DirecTV 500.

(Top) Arlus Schaefer of Warsaw, Ind., sent us this shot of himself and some buddies while attending Speedweeks 2000 at Daytona. From left are Mark Hamilton, Arlus, Michael Gunkel and Welsey Schaefer. (Above) Steve Trimm of Wichita, Kan., celebrates NASCAR 2000 in his own special way while relaxing in the motor home at Texas Motor Speedway. Terry Powers of Wichita, Kan., couldn't pass up the opportunity to take this picture we're sure Steve will treasure always. (Right) Tim and Stephanie McCormick of McInnville, Tenn., log one for the scrapbook. For this photo, Stephanie gave her camera to her father-in-law George Paquette, who did a nice job of showing us that everything is big at Talladega.

RACING

TOWARD

THE FUTURE

In the beginning, stock car racing actually meant racing cars that were stock. Jim Roper won NASCAR's first Strictly Stock race in 1949 when Glenn Dunnaway was disqualified. Dunnaway's crime? A set of reinforced rear springs to help his car withstand the stresses of racing. Today, the only pieces on a NASCAR Winston Cup Series stock car that can also be found on the street version of that model are the hood, roof and deck lid.

We've come a long way baby.

(Above Left) Neil Castles (06) watches the start of the race from the back of the pack as David Pearson (17) and Richard Petty (43) lead the field to the green flag at Asheville Speedway in 1967. (Below Left) Joe Weatherly drives on the old Beach and Road Course at Daytona Beach on February 19, 1957. Weatherly is in a DePaolo Engineering Ford. (Right) The garage at Darlington is packed full of cars with drivers hoping to put their sponsor in victory lane in this 1959 photo.

Rusty Wallace's Penske Racing Ford is about as sleek as they come, something that's quite standard in today's world of NASCAR Winston Cup Series racing.

The evolution of the NASCAR Winston Cup Series "stock"

but that pace is expected to slow over the next 50 years. NASCAR has hit upon the magic

them to upset the apple cart in that respect. Carbureted V8 engines, stock-appearing bodies

come, will affect everything else it takes to put on a race on Sunday.

car has been dramatic over the sport's first half-century,

formula — as far as cars go — that provides close, exciting racing, and nobody expects

and super-safe chassis and roll cage designs are here to stay. The changes, when they

In October of 1971, Bobby Allison (12) and Richard Petty (43) find themselves battling hard for position at Charlotte. There had been many battles between the two rivals before, and there would be many battles after this skirmish for position.

(Top) Bill Elliott (9) drops low and gains a position on Don Whittington (93) with Jody Ridley (90) trailing in hot pursuit at Darlington, S.C. (Above) Lake Speed (83) holds off Tommy Ellis (18) and Michael Waltrip (30) at Rockingham, N.C. (Left) Richard Petty (43) holds off Darrell Waltrip (88) at Atlanta in 1980. These larger "taxi cab" style cars were replaced in early 1981 by the still-standard 110-inch wheelbase machines.

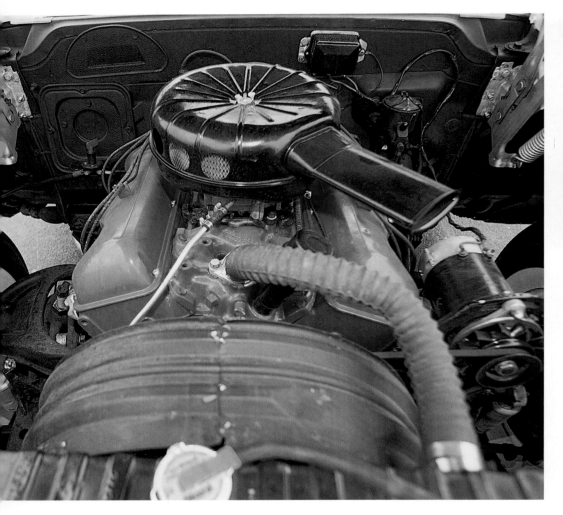

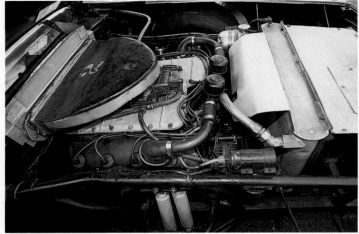

Engines in NASCAR Winston Cup Series racing have continued to evolve over the years as these motors from the 1950s (above left), 1960s (top) and 1970s (above) illustrate. Although the basic design has remained consistent over time (V-8, single-cam pushrod), these motors don't seem to bear much resemblance to the sophisticated powerplants of today, as shown at right.

(Right) The interior of a very early NASCAR ride was quite simple, with stripped-down bench seat and only a few bars in place to protect the driver. (Below) More bars fill the 1967 Ford Fairlane driven by Mario Andretti to the Daytona 500 win that year. Note the window crank still in place on the right side. (Opposite Page) By the mid 1960s, full door bars had become standard in stock cars, which were easy to photograph by opening the driver's-side door. Notice also the carpeted floor and the ignition keys hanging from the dash.

(Above Right) At today's tracks, elegance is the key word, as is the case with the Speedway Club and offices of Texas Motor Speedway. (Below Right) Condominiums like these that overlook the action at Atlanta Motor Speedway were once unheard of, but now have become very desirable and sought-after additions to modern superspeedways.

NASCAR Winston Cup Series racing hit its first boom phase when CBS

televised the Daytona 500 in its entirety for the first time to a live national audience in

1979. Since then, there have been such innovations as lighted superspeedways; luxury

suites; all-star and international races; NASCAR-themed restaurants, cartoons and

amusement parks; and even tracks willing to sell their names to add to the bottom line.

(Charlotte Motor Speedway became Lowe's Motor Speedway in 1999 for $35 million over

10 years.) Of course, old timers used to speedways being little more than dirt rings fash-

ioned in cow pastures might be more surprised to learn that a company would be willing

to pay good money to put its name on a track. By the way, there was no real end to the

first boom, the pace of things simply increased exponentially once the second boom hit.

(Right) The action in the NASCAR Craftsman Truck Series is as fierce and competitive as any, as demonstrated by this three-wide battle for position between Dennis Setzer (1), Lonnie Rush (27) and Randy Renfrow (41) at Daytona in February 2000. (Below) Veteran Mike Wallace (2) leads a host of hungry competitors on a restart at Daytona.

Many would argue that the obvious solution is to split the top Series into divisions so that it can race in two locations at once. But the sanctioning body's powers that be have from the beginning said that splitting NASCAR's most successful series isn't an option. Helton believes that splitting the NASCAR Winston Cup Series would not be the financial windfall many people expect.

Besides, NASCAR's top priority isn't making every last dollar possible; the top priority is to stay true to its roots and provide good, exciting racing to all its fans.

Martinsville Speedway is one of the showplace tracks in Virginia and guarantees some close, fender-to-fender action each time there are race cars on the track.

"I don't see NASCAR splitting the Series anytime in the near future," Helton says. "We've analyzed a lot of scenarios with an A and B league. None of them seemed to make sense as much as what has been working really well for us, which is having all the racers on one race track at one time. That's what we've been selling for the past 52 years. That includes selling the TV package as basically a Super Bowl every time we race, with the best there is competing against each other. We haven't found a scenario that does better than that right now.

"One of the reasons why we wouldn't want to do that is any division of what we do right now fragments things so much that the crowds and television audiences would stand a chance of not being bigger because the fans would be confused as to which they wanted to watch. So we like it the way it is now. Currently, there is more of a demand situation than we can supply, but that's just the way it is and we'll work around it the best we can."

(Left) Opened in 1969, Talladega Superspeedway is a slightly larger version of Daytona International Speedway, and has always been famous for packs of cars in tight drafts as was the case here, in May of 1993. (Far Left) The tight racing action of the early 1990s helped to set the foundation for today's close rivalries. Bobby Hillin (in aqua car) leads this group that includes Kenny Wallace (40), Bobby Labonte (22), Harry Gant (33), Hut Stricklin (27), Bobby Hamilton (68) and Dick Trickle (75).

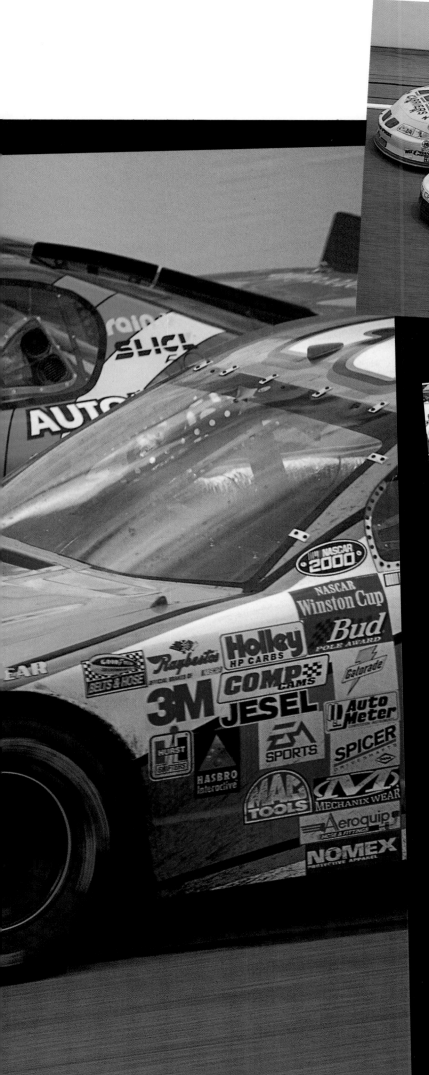

(Top) Up-and-comer Jerry Nadeau (1) takes the high side on seasoned veterans Dave Marcis (71) and Darrell Waltrip (17) at Daytona in July of 1997. (Above) Pit road is a busy place at every track on the circuit and is no exception at Charlotte in May of 1994. Competition in the pits can be just as important as that on the track, emphasizing the team aspect of NASCAR racing. (Left) When anticipating some of NASCAR's future rivalries, one needs to look no further than today's brightest young stars. Here, Jeff Gordon (24) and Tony Stewart (20) mix it up at Rockingham early in the 2000 NASCAR Winston Cup Series season.

Brett Bodine is one of the unlucky few who faces the threat of getting lost in the shuffle of this latest boom. An independent owner/driver in the NASCAR Winston Cup Series, Bodine has neither the financial backing nor the manpower to compete toe-to-toe with the mega-teams sprouting up like mushrooms across the NASCAR Winston Cup Series landscape.

Today, to field a team capable of winning only occasionally will cost upwards of eight million dollars. You also need a multi-car team willing to share information and split the skyrocketing costs of research and development — once you've squeezed the first 650 horses out of your engine program, every drop of additional horsepower costs drastically more than the last. To his credit, Bodine has been able to produce much more from his cash-strapped organization than anyone has a right to expect, but with the constantly growing level of competition, smaller teams might soon find themselves in over their heads.

Splitting the Series, however, could add life to those operations. Bodine could choose the series with the weaker competition and stand a chance at a good finish. Potential sponsors would also find the cost of supporting a team more manageable if the owner could guarantee that his car would make every race. Surprisingly, though, Bodine does not see a split as a viable option and thinks it would be a bad decision for everyone involved.

"Splitting the Winston Cup Series into two divisions is an option," he says, "but I don't think it would be successful. One of our sport's strong points is that we do compete with all our teams against each other at the same time. That's unlike most other sports where it's one on one. That's why when it becomes NCAA (basketball) Tournament time the excitement gets bigger, because that's when all the best teams are competing against each other at the same time.

"That's why playoff time in football and baseball also gets everybody so excited. The rest of the season is just kind of ho hum. One game doesn't mean a lot. But in our sport we hold the playoffs every weekend."

(Above) It takes tremendous resources to be competitive in the sport these days, including lots of engines. Teams often go through several motors on any given weekend. (Right) Three-time NASCAR Winston Cup Series Champion Jeff Gordon helps to push his car before the 2000 Daytona 500.

(Top) Team transporters arrive at the track each weekend carrying everything the team needs to compete, including two race cars and enough parts and pieces to rebuild them – if necessary. Here, the cars of Derrike Cope (36) and Kenny Wallace (81) are unloaded at California Speedway in 1997. (Above) Part of the allure of NASCAR Winston Cup Series racing is that the same stars show up to compete at each event. Here, the familiar cars of Rusty Wallace (2), Ricky Rudd (10) and Ted Musgrave (16) get service in the garage area at Charlotte in 1994.

Just as Helton and Bodine see the NASCAR Winston Cup Series staying the way it is, they both also feel the NASCAR Busch Series and NASCAR Craftsman Truck Series are perfectly placed in the pecking order. Both divisions are traditionally seen as feeder series for the NASCAR Winston Cup Series, which is fine. The goal is simply to make them more popular with fans. Both NASCAR Busch Series and NASCAR Craftsman Truck Series races feature some of the tightest, most intense racing out there, even if many of the drivers are still learning the ropes.

"We've made the decision that there will only be a single series of Cup racing, so trying to make the NASCAR Busch Series identical to Cup is not much different from having A and B leagues," Helton says. "Having said that, there is a place for the NASCAR Busch Series in motorsports, and we think that's second only to the NASCAR Winston Cup Series. And we'd like for the NASCAR Craftsman Truck Series to be third only to Cup and Busch in the whole industry of motorsports."

The NASCAR Craftsman Truck Series comes to full song in its debut at Daytona International Speedway in February of 2000. NASCAR's newest division provides race fans with yet another outlet to experience great race action, while also creating a breeding ground for future NASCAR stars.

"Understanding that, there are a lot more race tracks that desire a NASCAR Winston Cup race than Cup teams can afford to run," Helton points out. *"We've also got a supply and demand issue with the NASCAR Busch Series right now. Our intention is to keep the Busch Series healthy and make the Truck Series as healthy as the Busch Series so that we can supply some of the demand out there that we can't reach with either Busch or Cup. We have no master plan to make the Busch or Truck Series comparable to Winston Cup. There is only one NASCAR Winston Cup Series out there, and we want to keep it that way. The NASCAR Busch Series has value and personality in its own right that is second only to Cup, and we are eager to make the Truck Series as promising as the Busch Series is. That's where our concerted effort is today."*

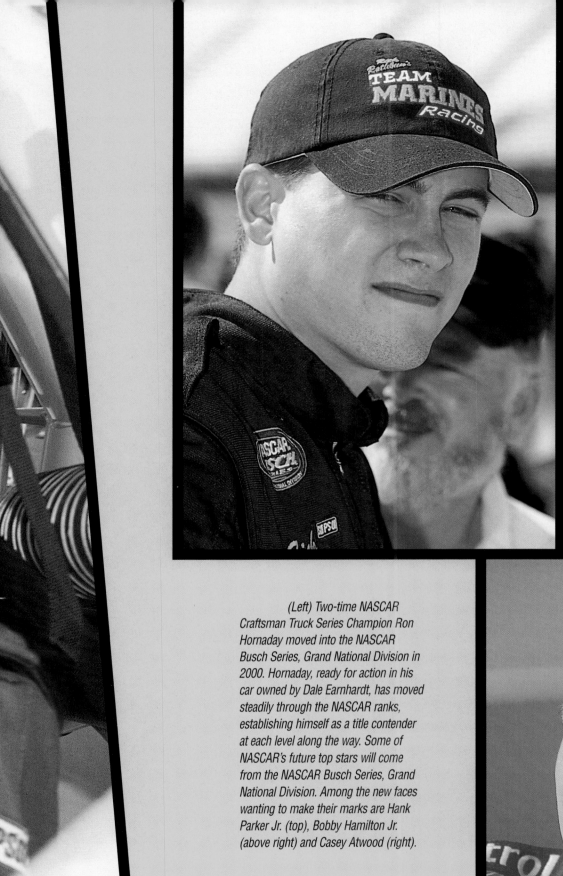

(Left) Two-time NASCAR Craftsman Truck Series Champion Ron Hornaday moved into the NASCAR Busch Series, Grand National Division in 2000. Hornaday, ready for action in his car owned by Dale Earnhardt, has moved steadily through the NASCAR ranks, establishing himself as a title contender at each level along the way. Some of NASCAR's future top stars will come from the NASCAR Busch Series, Grand National Division. Among the new faces wanting to make their marks are Hank Parker Jr. (top), Bobby Hamilton Jr. (above right) and Casey Atwood (right).

So if the plan isn't to change the format but, instead, grow all three series into even bigger events, the question becomes, how big can it all get?

NASCAR Winston Cup Series racing has already become a spectacle in itself. Most tracks with a Cup date annually draw the largest single-day sporting event crowd in their respective state. For comparison, even the most poorly attended races rival professional football crowds.

Fans travel incredible distances and reserve precious vacation time to attend races at their favorite tracks. The assemblage of souvenir hawkers, food vendors, product promoters and campers in their brightly colored trailers, trucks and vans create a unique atmosphere — somewhere between an old-style carnival and small-town America. Where else can you cook your steak on a stranger's grill and be offered a drink in the process?

(Left) A huge crowd packs the grandstands for the NASCAR Winston Cup Series' triumphant return to Texas in the inaugural event at Texas Motor Speedway in 1997. (Right, Above) There is no lack of enthusiasm in the infield during race weekend, as demonstrated by this group of fans at Pocono. (Right, Below) Shopping along "souvenir row" is always a favorite pastime among fans while attending a NASCAR event. (Below) One enthusiastic fan sends a clear message as to how she feels about her favorite driver.

You can thank NASCAR for all of this. Before Bill France Sr. stepped in to bring some organization to the world of stock car racing in 1948, promoters were as likely to skip town with the purse as they were to pay the drivers their winnings. Events were sparsely attended and usually devoid of women. (Race tracks often lacked facilities.) The culture of racing in the South had a rogue reputation and was generally considered only slightly better than cockfighting and back-alley gambling.

France brought legitimacy to stock car racing when he began promoting several series under the NASCAR umbrella. Rulings were consistent (at least compared to what drivers had earlier faced) and purses were paid as promised. Although it would still be many years before racing could provide a living for more than the top few drivers, NASCAR made steady progress and growth under the France family's control.

(Above) Bill Elliott (in car) gets a few thoughts from Ray Evernham (in light shirt) during a practice session in Atlanta in March of 2000. The popular veteran will join Evernham – a star in his own right – fielding Dodges in 2001. (Right) Ricky Craven (41) leads Bobby Hamilton (43) in the opening laps of an event at New Hampshire International Speedway in 1996. The one-mile oval joined the NASCAR Winston Cup Series in 1993, giving New England fans a new venue to enjoy.

So where does it go from here? By the time you read this, a proposed 24-hour NASCAR channel may already be broadcasting. Or maybe the NASCAR Winston Cup Series will be racing in New York and Chicago — geographically and ideologically a pretty long way from Darlington, S.C. Maybe pay-per-view options will allow you to watch an entire race from your favorite driver's car. Many of those in the know say it is only a matter of time before all three possibilities are old news. Helton says whatever comes next, NASCAR will move deliberately to make sure it doesn't shortchange its fans for the sake of the almighty dollar. He's hesitant to either boast or put a limit on how big NASCAR can become.

"I don't know how big it can get," he says diplomatically. "I don't know if there's a dimension out there that you can say, 'This is it.' We have to be careful and very mindful about growth. We have to stay conscious of the fact that this (phenomenal growth) isn't going to be this way forever. So we have to do all the smart things we can to keep it growing but, at the same time, keep it what everybody is used to. And that's difficult; it's our biggest concern today.

"The biggest pitfall we have to avoid is the perception that NASCAR is a large, greedy monster that is only looking for what it can gobble up next. I think that's a perception that we have to work on and try to get the real story out a little bit stronger. We are interested in keeping our feet planted and not just trying to grow every time we turn the corner. We have to stay conscious of the desires of our current fans."

Given the current size of NASCAR and its three major series, there is an army of drivers, owners, officials, vendors and sundry other support personnel that depend on the success of the sanctioning body to earn a living. When you count all the dollars involved — everything from race tickets, to construction crews working on another race shop, to car dealers selling new Chevrolet Monte Carlos after Jeff Gordon wins on Sunday — NASCAR is a multi-billion dollar business, and it's all family owned and operated. To NASCAR's credit, those involved in the sport for a living are largely happy with the way it's going.

(Above) The garage area is buzzing with activity prior to the start of the 2000 Daytona 500. (Left) An early morning sun reflects off the multi-colored machines of the NASCAR Craftsman Truck Series prior to a full day of activity at Martinsville.

Crew chief Jimmy Fennig (left) listens to his driver, Mark Martin, during a break at Martinsville in 1999. Strong communication between driver and crew chief is perhaps the most important ingredient in winning at NASCAR's top level of competition.

"Right now, I feel like we've got some tremendously talented people steering this ship between Mike Helton, Gary Nelson (director of the NASCAR Winston Cup Series) and their respective staffs," Bodine says. "And there's Brian France (senior vice president) on the marketing side. I think they all are doing a great job. They have to make sure the growth doesn't happen too fast, and it doesn't happen too slow. There is a delicate balance. I'm sure they could just let this thing run rampant, but they've got to make sure they don't do anything that could hurt the sport in the long run.

"I don't envy their jobs because they've got a lot of decisions to make, and you've got to be a fortune teller of sorts. You've got to see into the future, and you've got to keep an eye on what the economy is going to be like. Right now I think the sport can get as big as it wants to; there are a lot of areas of the country that would love to have Winston Cup racing and could support it. So the demand is greater than the supply, which is in favor of helping the sport stay healthy."

H.A. "Humpy" Wheeler, Lowe's Motor Speedway's vice president, is also confident in the sport's growth. Wheeler is a marketer extraordinaire and widely considered a visionary when it comes to NASCAR Winston Cup Series racing. He and Bruton Smith, president of Speedway Motorsports, the company that owns the track, made LMS the first to offer lighted racing at a superspeedway, condos overlooking a race track and a private dinner club. Wheeler has seen it all and doesn't hesitate to offer his vision when it comes to NASCAR's future.

(Above) Davey Allison (28) leads the field across the start-finish line to begin The Winston at Charlotte in 1992. It was the first time the sport's all-star race had been run under the lights, and what was dubbed "One Hot Night" ended in a shower of sparks with Kyle Petty and Allison banging and spinning while taking the checkered flag. (Opposite Page) Three-time NASCAR Winston Cup Series Champion Darrell Waltrip takes a moment to reflect at Texas in March of 1999.

"I think it will become a global sport," he says. "I think it will leave this country and go to Europe and the Pacific Rim. I think we will have other makes of cars in it besides Ford, Chevy, Pontiac and Chrysler. I think we'll see BMW, Mercedes, etc. I think we'll see drivers from outside the United States competing in it also. So I'm looking at it as the real potential is globally."

Both Wheeler and Helton agree that the key to continued growth won't be marketing or expansion into new tracks in untapped areas. That's all important, but everything is based on the product, which is good, exciting racing. Good racing is defined as lots of passing and close finishes, usually under green. Fast is nice, but it doesn't count for much if it makes the drivers so uncomfortable they are afraid to pass. Wheeler recommends making the drivers a greater factor in the outcome of the race by giving them slower cars that stick to the track like glue. Theoretically, that would give the drivers confidence to race like it was the last lap the entire event. Smaller carburetors and more drag-inducing downforce should do the trick.

"I'm all for slowing the cars down," he says, "particularly at the mile and mile-and-a-half tracks. I think that would help the competition a lot. Here's the problem: Daytona and Talladega are relatively easy tracks to drive. California and Michigan are relatively easy to drive. When you get to the mile-and-a-half tracks and under, the Charlottes, the Darlingtons, the Dovers, etc., it demands a great deal of driving skill and handling. If the drivers are uncomfortable in the race cars, then it's going to make passing more difficult. That means you won't have the drama that you need."

Fast or slow, there is no denying that NASCAR racing, especially its Winston Cup division, has reached the realm of the big three in professional sports: football, basketball and baseball. It is sometimes difficult to group racing with stick-and-ball sports because it is so unique in so many ways, but when you boil it down to the bare bones, it's all about entertainment — and NASCAR has done an outstanding job of providing fans with what they are looking for. There has been a lot of racing come down the pipe since Ben Hur took the checkers in his chariot, and since then our appetite to see who can be the first from here to there has only increased. NASCAR has done the best job of providing good racing between drivers we find easy to root for, and the response has been a multitude of fans that live and breathe racing. For 52 years NASCAR has provided good times and great racing, and it shows no signs of letting up anytime soon.

Here's to the future.

(Above) 1989 champion Rusty Wallace watches the competition as the 2000 season begins at Daytona. (Right) Pole-winner Jeff Gordon (24) and outside front-row starter Joe Nemechek (41) lead the field at Charlotte in 1994. Later that evening, Gordon notched his first career NASCAR Winston Cup Series win, thus beginning a dominating run that brought him three championships over four seasons.

UMI publishes the NASCAR Preview and Press Guide. For subscription information call 704-374-0420 or visit our website at www.umipub.com.